Autobiography of

JOHN RUSSELL BARTLETT

AUTOBIOGRAPHY OF

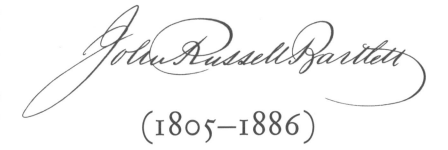

(1805–1886)

Edited by

JERRY E. MUELLER

PROVIDENCE, RHODE ISLAND

THE JOHN CARTER BROWN LIBRARY

2006

Correspondence should be directed to:
THE JOHN CARTER BROWN LIBRARY
BOX 1894, PROVIDENCE, RHODE ISLAND 02912
ADDITIONAL INFORMATION MAY BE
FOUND AT WWW.JCBL.ORG

Frontispiece:
Adapted from an engraving of Bartlett
based on the R. A. Lewis photograph of
ca. 1875. The engraving appeared first as
a plate following page 128 of the *Russell
Family Genealogy* (1879)

★

THE JOHN CARTER BROWN LIBRARY IS
AN INDEPENDENTLY FUNDED AND ADMINISTERED
INSTITUTION FOR ADVANCED RESEARCH IN HISTORY AND
THE HUMANITIES, FOUNDED IN 1846 AND
LOCATED AT BROWN UNIVERSITY SINCE 1901

CONTENTS

LIST OF ILLUSTRATIONS

PREFACE

THOUSANDS of historical manuscripts sit in libraries around the world awaiting their champions, those who will rescue them from oblivion. Reading and interpreting old manuscripts requires passion, far more than is the case with printed books, although they, too, may languish forgotten. The determined student of a historical manuscript must contend, usually, with barely legible handwriting, disorganization in the surviving text, gaps in the record, and fragmentary evidence.

John Russell Bartlett's brief autobiographical memoir found its champion from a most unlikely source. The editor of this volume did not come from a history or an English department in academe, or any humanistic discipline. Prof. Jerry E. Mueller is a geomorphologist by training, a student of the description and analysis of landforms. We speak metaphorically in the humanities about "unearthing" evidence, and "digging" for sources, but beyond this borrowing of language, the connection with geological science appears slim. How did Mueller find his way to the John Carter Brown Library?

The answer is terrain, specifically the landscapes of New Mexico, Arizona, Texas, California, etc. Bartlett was an accomplished bookman—a lexicographer, a bibliographer, a documentary editor, a historian, and more—but for that achievement he has been largely forgotten. To this day he is widely remembered only as a highly skilled artist of the Southwest, whose surviving watercolors and drawings in the early 1850s of that territory where Mexico and the United

States now meet have been widely acclaimed for their documentary value.

Bartlett was in the Southwest as head of the U.S. section of the commission that ran the boundary between the United States and Mexico following the Treaty of Guadalupe Hidalgo, and he seized the opportunity—as he did numerous others in his full life—to make a contribution to knowledge. We have in the John Carter Brown Library over 200 of his drawings, and they have not rested in obscurity. In 1968 Robert V. Hine published *Bartlett's West* (Yale University Press) in which Hine reproduced more than 50 of Bartlett's drawings, but without any attempt to link Bartlett's sketches and paintings with the exact location of the view depicted. There could be no doubt that Bartlett was capturing a real place and was painting what he saw. He was always the documentarian and had no interest in fantasies. But it was not always evident precisely where the site was. How could Hine and others know that the scene Bartlett himself described as the "Big Horn Mountain" is actually a view of the northern extremity of the Mohawk Mountains, fifty-one miles east-northeast of Yuma, Arizona, or that his depiction of "Fording a stream. Pack mules sink in a quicksand," is a scene located along Sonoita Creek, near Patagonia, Arizona?

Professor Mueller knows the Southwest landscape intimately, from years of roaming that terrain as a scientist, and one of his interests is landform evolution. In 1970 he was engaged in research on the changes over time in the channel of the Rio Grande along the international boundary and came upon John Russell Bartlett's two-volume, illustrated classic account of the work of the Boundary Commission,

Personal Narrative (1854). Bartlett's drawings therein contain geological and topographical information, but to make use of that data one first has to know where Bartlett was when he made the drawing.

When Mueller began his investigation of the Bartlett drawings more than a decade ago, he soon realized that much of the available information on this visual record was inaccurate and that much work remained to be done to determine exactly where Bartlett was at the artistic moment. Scientists and historians have in common a desire to get their facts straight; so Professor Mueller undertook to identify Bartlett's precise vantage point for nearly every image. In 2000 he published the results in *An Annotated Guide to the Artwork of the United States Boundary Commission, 1850–1853, Under the Direction of John Russell Bartlett* (Las Cruces, N.Mex.).

Happily, Professor Mueller did not let his contribution rest there. To identify the drawings properly, he drew on all of the documentary evidence he could find, becoming closely acquainted with Bartlett's paper legacy, in print and manuscript, not only at the John Carter Brown Library and Brown University but also at the Rhode Island Historical Society and the Providence Athenaeum.

We at the John Carter Brown Library share Professor Mueller's enthusiasm for Bartlett, and equally wished to see the man's lifetime of accomplishment resuscitated and recognized. When Professor Mueller offered to prepare an annotated edition of Bartlett's memoir, we leaped at the idea of seeing documented for posterity a good part of Bartlett's lifetime of quiet achievement.

The work is finished, and it is impressive to me that a geomorphologist could so successfully metamorphose into a skilled historian, taking on all of the virtues of the professional: thoroughness, attention to detail, the mustering of evidence, artful characterization.

There is little need here for me to say much about Bartlett and why he deserves this book-length treatment. His importance is evident from even the most cursory browse through this volume. Bartlett was one of those amazingly industrious nineteenth-century bookmen with a long list of accomplishments to his name who will never get his due. Gentlemen in that era did not court publicity for its own sake, and the genus *media celebrity*, famous for being famous, had not yet emerged. The closest Bartlett ever came to self-promotion was the spare and brief autobiography we are publishing here, left only in manuscript more than a century ago.

At the John Carter Brown Library we are intensely conscious of our institutional history, going back for 160 years, and Bartlett was a formative figure in that history. A portrait of him hangs in this building (see fig. 12, below), and the staff regularly has occasion to consult his pioneering catalogues of John Carter Brown's collection, the *Bibliotheca Americana*, a series that Bartlett initiated in 1865. These catalogues set a high standard for presentation of the records of the Library's holdings that we have adhered to ever since.

One senses in Bartlett an omnivorous interest in, and appreciation of, all matters historical, from the humble to the grand, which may have been the source of John Carter Brown's unusual commitment to acquiring the *totality* of what was printed in, or about, the Western Hemisphere from the time of Columbus to 1800. Bartlett's compiling of a *Dictionary of Americanisms* (1848) indicates his fascination with language outside of standard English, and his contribution to the founding of the American Ethnological Society reveals his attention not only to European and American heroes but also to indigenous peoples

The preparation of this publication owes much to the Library's in-house editor, Nan Sumner-Mack, and to the close reading of the manuscript that Prof. Rob Emlen provided at an early stage. The cost of design, typesetting, and manufacture has been underwritten in part by the Maurice L. Clemence Publications Fund at the JCB.

INTRODUCTION

JOHN RUSSELL BARTLETT (1805–1886) had a colorful and multi-faceted career that included periods as a merchant, a bank cashier, a book dealer, an author and publisher, a United States Boundary Commissioner, the Rhode Island Secretary of State, and a librarian. He was an intellectual whose interests and expertise spanned many disciplines, although he is best known for his contributions as a bibliographer and ethnographer. In addition, Bartlett was a founder and/or member of numerous local, state, and national organizations, societies, and commissions. In all these endeavors he had a strong sense of history and of the need to collect, compile, catalogue, and preserve the past. As a result, Bartlett himself has become a historical figure. The engraving of Bartlett that appears as the frontispiece of this work, dating from approximately 1875, also appears in the *Dictionary of American Portraits* (1967) by Howard and Blanche Cirker, an indication of the notability Bartlett acquired during and after his lifetime.

Bartlett was born in 1805 into a family of merchants in Providence, Rhode Island. As business opportunities for his father developed elsewhere, young Bartlett moved with his family several times, although for the better part of his youth he was raised and educated in Kingston, Ontario. His formal education ended at age seventeen after two years at an academy in upstate New York and one year under a private tutor in Montreal. Unlike his father and brothers, who spent most of their lives in communities along the U.S.-Canadian border, Bartlett returned to Providence in 1824. He worked in his maternal uncle's dry-goods store for four years, followed by a total of eight years of employment in two different Providence banks. During these Providence years, Bartlett developed a network of friends and acquaintances from among the professional ranks, many of whom were men of wealth and influence. Although never wealthy himself, at least prior to the 1860s, the enormously talented and energetic Bartlett was able to win the confidence of those who would eventually support many of his civic and professional activities.

Among Bartlett's greatest achievements was his cofounding of the Providence Athenaeum in 1831, an organization that within five years would absorb the much older Providence Library Company. He was active in all phases of the Athenaeum's development, serving as an officer and as a member of many committees; writing numerous committee reports; purchasing and cataloguing books; raising funds for a new building; and so forth. At about the same time, Bartlett became very active in the local Franklin Society and the Rhode Island Historical Society, writing and delivering numerous public lectures on a variety of subjects related to ethnology and archaeology. He also pursued his passion for drawing and painting, a talent that would serve him well for the next fifty years.

Bartlett moved to New York in 1836 and worked in a commission house until 1840. He was instrumental in the resurrection of the New-York Historical Society in the late 1830s, while at the same time adding to his large circle of influential friends, which included Albert Gallatin. As his business venture largely failed following the national financial crisis of the late 1830s, Bartlett began to sell books on consignment in order to supplement his income. In 1840, he formed a partnership with a young Englishman, Charles Welford, and the two men operated a bookstore in Manhattan until Bartlett's departure from the city in 1849. Also during the 1840s, Bartlett co-founded the very successful American Ethnological Society; held a number of literary and scientific soirees at his house; published his first two books, *Progress of Ethnology* and *Dictionary of Americanisms*; and unsuccessfully sought a diplomatic post in Europe.

In 1850, the Whig administration under Zachary Taylor appointed Bartlett the U.S. Commissioner on the Mexican Boundary Survey. Bartlett was delighted at the opportunity to serve in a Federal position, one that would allow him to travel extensively and to pursue his major interest in ethnology—the North American Indian. However, the commission under Bartlett was racked with internal dissension; major periodic changes in senior-level personnel; the failure in Washington to secure Congressional approval for a compromise boundary line for southern and western New Mexico; a lack of adequate supplies for the survey teams in the field; and overspending that resulted in a major budget deficit. Congress held Bartlett accountable for these many problems, and in March 1853, under the new Democratic administration of Franklin Pierce, Bartlett was dismissed. Despite these failures, much of the international boundary, as defined in the Treaty of Guadalupe Hidalgo of 1848, was surveyed, mapped, and marked during Bartlett's tenure on the commission. In 1854, Bartlett published an account of his travels and observations in the American Southwest—a two-volume book, *Personal Narrative*, considered by many to be a classic that ranks alongside the works of other, more acclaimed, western explorers of the period.

Bartlett became Rhode Island's Secretary of State in 1855, a position he held until 1872. During that period, he organized and published many of the state's colonial records; published volumes related to the Civil War; and obtained, at no cost to the state, an extensive collection of portraits of early Rhode Island leaders. In approximately 1855, he began his long period of service as private librarian to John Carter Brown and the Brown family, a position he held until his death in 1886. For bibliophiles, Bartlett's greatest achievement is the series of catalogues he produced of the Bibliotheca Americana, John Carter Brown's personal book collection, which ultimately would become a world-class research library—the John Carter Brown Library on the campus of Brown University.

Bartlett continued to be very productive after 1872. He published additional catalogues of the Bibliotheca Americana; produced a genealogy of his mother's family, the Russells; published a history of the Wanton family of Newport, Rhode Island; and edited the letters of Roger Williams. After the death of John Carter Brown in 1874, Bartlett worked closely with Brown's widow, Sophia Augusta, and the Browns' two sons, John Nicholas Brown and Harold Brown, to further develop the Bibliotheca Americana. In 1880, Bartlett donated his Mexican Boundary Survey papers to the Bibliotheca Americana, including more than 200 drawings made by Bartlett and others of sites they had visited in the Southwest. He also continued to draw and paint, as evidenced by a large collection of his watercolors, some dated as late as 1880, that are held by the Rhode Island Historical Society. Another of Bartlett's passions was collecting printed graphics that he could use to grangerize, or extra-illustrate, books. Of the books he is known to have extra-illustrated, Bartlett took what were originally thirty-one volumes and extended them to at least sixty-eight volumes.

Bartlett seems to have become a largely forgotten man after approximately 1900. His name did not resurface until historians, beginning in the 1950s, began to look more closely at nineteenth-century explorations in the Southwest. This was followed in the 1960s by the rediscovery of Bartlett's Boundary Commission drawings at the John Carter Brown Library. Perhaps nothing rekindled more interest in Bartlett than the reissue of his *Personal Narrative* in 1965. Thereafter, Bartlett became more widely known among both academics and lay people, and several books have appeared that discuss the significance of Bartlett's travels and artwork in the Southwest. Today, Bartlett is a more recognizable figure in American history, and his accomplishments are looked upon very favorably in parts of the country, especially, and understandably, the Northeast. In the Southwest, however, Bartlett's failings as Boundary Commissioner often tend to overshadow his many other accomplishments, and in that region, he is destined to remain a controversial figure. It is most unfortunate that some writers have embellished Bartlett's record to the point where it becomes very difficult to sort fact from fiction!

John Russell Bartlett's handwritten autobiography was crafted in three distinct stages. The first part covers the period from his birth in 1805 to the year 1867 and forms the bulk of the work. The second section goes to approximately 1872 and emphasizes Bartlett's trip to Europe in 1867. The third portion was written in approximately 1885, shortly before his death, and includes coverage of Bartlett's second trip to Europe in 1872, plus a few anecdotes he forgot to include in the earlier sections. Regrettably, Bartlett's treatment of his life after 1867 is much less detailed than the period before. As a result, there is little information about the later years when he served as Rhode Island's Secretary of State, and there is virtually nothing about the important service he rendered for many years as private librarian to John Carter Brown and the Brown family. Known for his industriousness and gentlemanly disposition, Bartlett also had a reputation for honesty and humility; he makes little mention of the recognition and awards that came his way in the middle and later stages of his life.

I have made every effort to reproduce the manuscript faithfully. Bartlett did not carefully proof or edit previously written sections to make major changes and corrections; thus his punctuation is sometimes either odd or missing, and these idiosyncrasies are left as they appear in the original text. Even Bartlett's footnotes, indicated by asterisks rather than by numbers, are left intact, with the footnote information placed at the bottom of the respective pages. The reader will also detect some redundancies, misspellings, and the occasional use of archaic forms of words in Bartlett's writing. Another facet of the original document is that the legibility of Bartlett's handwriting decreased in his advanced years, and the style and format of his writing in 1885 is far more tortured than his earlier efforts. Had Bartlett, the experienced author, known that his autobiography was to be published, his final product would have been far different than the one presented here.

My brief notes and emendations within the text are bracketed, and the additional explanatory or extended notes are numbered consecutively and appear as endnotes. Also included within brackets are the page numbers of the original manuscript. The illustrations, none of which were part of the original autobiography, are mostly grouped and are inserted strategically throughout the text for the interest of the reader. These figures have been gathered from a wide variety of sources and constitute the largest assemblage of portraits of Bartlett ever published in a single volume.

ACKNOWLEDGMENTS

THIS VOLUME would have been impossible to produce without the assistance provided by a great number of individuals and organizations. First and foremost is the staff at the John Carter Brown Library, who afforded me access to the John Russell Bartlett Papers, including the original handwritten autobiography of Bartlett that is the subject of this book. In particular, Norman Fiering, Director and Librarian; Susan Danforth, Assistant Librarian for Library Operations and Curator of Maps and Prints; Richard Hurley, Fine Art Photographer; and Richard Ring, Reference and Acquisitions Librarian, were all helpful and hospitable during the many phases of this project. Their kindness and that of their colleagues is very much appreciated.

Significant contributions have been made to this project by the following organizations and their listed staff members: Brown University—Raymond Butti, Jr., Robert Emlen, Gayle Lynch, Ronald Potvin, Jean Rainwater, and Holly Snyder; the Providence Athenaeum—Jonathan Bengston and Lee Teverow; the Rhode Island Historical Society—Jeanne Creighton, Allison Cywin, Bernard Fishman, Kirsten Hammerstrom, and Rick Stattler; Rhode Island State Government—Ernest Balasco, Kenneth Carlson, Evan Duncan, and Thomas Evans; Arizona State University—Malcolm Comeaux and Jeremy Rowe; New Mexico Bureau of Geology—David Love and Jane Love.

Among the other individuals who contributed to the research on this volume are: Bernard Bell, Providence, RI; Andreas Brown, New York, NY; Patrick Conley, East Providence, RI; Manuel DaSilva, Bristol, RI; Margaret and Richard Gummere, Jr., Barrytown, NY; John Haskell, Jr., College of William & Mary; Tom Jonas, Phoenix, AZ; Elizabeth Loeffler, University of Bristol; Jeffrey McNairn, Queen's University; David Miller, Cameron University; John Myers, Providence City Archives; Keith O'Malley, Squantum Association; Tory Perrotta, Westminster Unitarian Church, East Greenwich, RI; Clare Rogan, the Rhode Island School of Design; Diane Swanson, the United States Sanitary Commission; C. R. Twidale, University of Adelaide; and Phil Weimerskirch, Providence Public Library.

Special credit is due Kate Wodehouse, Technical Services Librarian at the Providence Athenaeum, for her magnanimous contribution of research and illustrative material. In addition, she provided many useful sources of uncatalogued material located in the Athenaeum's archives. And for keeping this project on schedule, thanks are due to Dana Munroe, Registrar and Graphics Curator at the Rhode Island Historical Society Library, who made manuscript material available at a time when that agency was in the throes of major personnel changes and reorganization. I am also indebted to Steve Welch, Las Cruces, New Mexico, who generously provided digital imaging support for this and several other Bartlett-related projects.

For assistance in all phases of this project, especially in reading and deciphering the more difficult sections of Bartlett's original text, the valuable service of Geraldine Mueller is acknowledged. She also provided editorial support, as well as research assistance in the library and in the field. Less tangible but significant support has come from: Daniel Blumenfeld; Charles Eyer; Ray Henkel; Harold James; Lois and William King; Sam Moore, Jr.; Albert Peters; Mark Walters; Carl William Wegner, Jr.; and the following Muellers—Wade and Shelley; Wayland and Jennifer; Devin and Mason; Robert and Susan, and Alex.

Autobiography of

JOHN RUSSELL BARTLETT

Autobiography of
JOHN RUSSELL BARTLETT

[*This portion of the autobiography appears to have been written in 1867.*]

[1] At the particular request of my wife and children I write the following incidents in my life from my birth; this little and unimportant record being for their especial use.

I was born in Providence, Rhode Island on the 23d of October 1805. My father was Smith Bartlett, living while I write this, at Cape Vincent, New York. He was born in April 1780. My mother was Nancy, daughter of John Russell, the son of Thomas, who came from Boston to Providence in the early part of the 18th century.[1]

My father was the son of Rufus Bartlett and was born in Cumberland, R. I. My father's brothers and sisters were Abner; Phila, married Dr. Lamb, of Grafton, Mass; & Anne, married Geo. Ballou, of Cumberland, R. I. My grandfather [great-grandfather] was Abner Bartlett, who also lived in Cumberland or Smithfield.[2]

[2] My mother's brothers and sisters will be found in the annexed note★ [*none provided*].[3]

While an infant my father removed to Utica, New York, then called "the West," where he remained but a short time. Believing that a better opening for business existed in Upper

★ Brothers and sisters of my mother. See Russell Genealogy.[3]

Canada he removed to Kingston [Ontario], after but a few months stay in Utica, and established himself in business as a merchant.[4] This must have been in the year 1807.[5]

[1806–1824, Kingston, Ontario]

The earliest school that I remember to have attended was kept by Mrs. Trimmer, and was what we would now call an infant's school. I was then six years old. When I grew older I was sent to a school kept by William Moon, an Englishman, whose pleasant genial face is still strongly impressed on my mind. He was rather an aged [3] man, and married one of his former pupils, which made a good deal of talk at the time.

When the war of 1812 with Great Britain broke out all Americans were required to leave Canada within a stipulated period, or take the oath of allegiance to His Majesty George 3d. My father's business was then much extended, so that, to close it up suddenly and leave the province would have been attended with serious loss, if not total ruin. He therefore determined to remain and continue his business, which, at that time, was the most extensive of any merchant in Upper Canada. All his goods were purchased by him in Montreal, where he made frequent visits. Merchandize was then transported on the St. Lawrence in Canadian batteaux, which were large open boats rowed by eight or ten men. It was a long and tedious voyage up the river in these boats, which always came in numbers of from five to twenty. When they returned empty, with the aid of the current, the voyage was made about four days. In the winter merchandize was brought from Montreal in Canadian sleighs, called by them "trains," [4] or in French "traineaux." These were drawn by a single horse, and could not, therefore, carry much. Two crates of crockery, or a single cask of Jamaica rum (the common spirituous liquor then drank) made a load. Sometimes during the winter twenty of these teams filled with merchandize would arrive for my father, the arrival of which would cause as much sensation as the arrival of a great ocean steamer did the first years of their crossing the Atlantic. In those days merchants did not, as now, confine themselves to one description of merchandize, but they dealt in everything. I remember that my father kept Dry Goods, Groceries, Liquors, Hardware, Flour, Crockery, Iron and Steel, Saddles, Boots and Shoes, Paper and Stationery, in fact, every kind of merchandize required in the country.

I remember what delight it gave me to help my father open his numerous boxes of new goods, particularly the crates of crockery that contained toys. He used to promise us that if we were good children we [could] sit up an hour or two in the evening to help him open his new goods. My brother William and I once used our spending money in buying toys in Montreal [5] which we resold at retail, deriving therefrom a handsome profit. With the money made on these toys after several operations, we bought a set of silver spoons which we presented to our mother. On one occasion during the war my father lost about ten thousand dollars value in merchandize in batteaux coming up the St. Lawrence, taken by the U.S. forces. The goods were taken to Ogdensburgh [New York], and although he went there personally to recover them, and a promise was made him that, being private property they should be restored, he was never able to obtain them.

I remember distinctly many events of the war, although I was but seven years of age when it broke out. It absorbed the whole attention of the people as Kingston, the chief town, was exposed to an attack both by land and water. Reports constantly came in that the American fleet would attack it. Kingston was then, and is still a strongly fortified place, protected chiefly by Fort Henry, which stands on an elevated point of land opposite the town, its guns commanding the harbor. The town was enclosed with stakes or pickets, and palisades; and [6] entrances were through gates leading to the principal streets. These gates were protected by Blockhouses, the lower part of which were of stone and the upper or projecting parts of heavy timber. Some of these blockhouses were standing a few years since, and may be still. A large military force was kept at Kingston during the war, the barracks for which were in the lower part of the town near the river, now enclosed by a high stone wall. This was an old French Fort, and was known as Fort Frontenac. I remember when a boy that there were many remains of the old fort, particularly a circular stone building stuccoed with plaster and gravel, called the powder magazine. This building was afterwards torn down. On one occasion when an increased force of soldiers came to the town, [I remember] that they were billeted on the inhabitants. I remember well that a British officer was billeted on our family. He was a gentlemanly man and made himself quite agreeable to the family.

On the [blank] the American fleet entered the harbor of Kingston and created the greatest consternation. They bombarded the town [7] during the whole day; but the guns at Fort Henry kept the ships so far off that little if any damage was done. I do not remember that any one was killed in Kingston. My father took his musket and with other citizens went a few miles into the interior to protect the town from

attack in that quarter. Our [family] on the morning of the
day of the bombardment, that is, my mother and her children, went to the house of Mr. Alcott, who kept a tavern in
Store Street, on the north side, being the stone house next
above that of Mr. Heath, the druggist. I distinctly remember the roar of the artillery the whole of the day. From the
top of the house, we could see the enemy's fleet; and when
they took their departure towards evening, all firing ceased
and our family and many others who had sought safety
there, returned home.[6] My father then lived in a two story
wooden house on the corner of what was then Store Street
(now Princess) and King Street. (I think was the name of the
street that intersected it) It is the south-west corner and
opposite to the corner house now belonging to my cousin [8]
Mrs. R. M. Rose. We occupied this same house during the
war and for some time previous.

The house opposite was a low wooden one of one story
built of wood and painted red. There lived a Mr. Demill
[Anthony Demill], who married my mother's sister Amy
Russell [Amey Russell] who lived with us. Upon his death
not long after she married Captain George Smith, an English
Naval Officer, who commanded one of the British ships at
Kingston during the war. By her second marriage she had a
daughter Amy [Amey], who, upon growing up, became the
wife of Mr. Roderick M. Rose, a Scotsman, of Kingston, by
whom she had a large family of children, most of which are
now living in or near Kingston. Much of Mrs. Rose's early
life was passed in our family, hence she seemed very near to
us all, and is regarded still by us with feelings of affection.*

* The children of Mrs. Rose are George Smith [George Smith
Rose] who served in the U.S. Army during the rebellion. Married

[9] Mr. Demill, having no children, left all his property to his wife, which has since become very valuable. Some of his relatives soon after his death made an effort to recover it but were unsuccessful.

At the close of the war, in the year 1816 or 17, my father determined to leave Canada and settle in the city of New York. He accordingly removed there with his family. He took a house in Brooklyn, where we lived some six months, and where his children attended school. New York then had a population of [approximately 200,000]. On several occasions when I went over to the city, I made bold to venture up Broadway to Canal Street, which then appeared to be on the limits. A small stream then ran down Canal Street, over which was a bridge. I remember standing on this bridge and looking towards the North River. Our family, after a brief residence in Brooklyn, came to Providence to visit the family of my uncle William Russell, who then lived on the corner of Star and Benefit Street. Leaving his family here, my father went to Canada to close up his business. Finding business active and the [10] country prosperous, he purchased some valuable property in Kingston, in Front Street, and determined to return there with his family and resume business. Soon after we all returned to Kingston. In 1819, Feb. 11, my mother died, leaving six children, all she ever had.[7]

I now went to the school of Mr. Baxter, then the principal school in Kingston. About a year after when about 13 or 14 years of age, William, my elder brother, and myself were

---

Mary L. Israel of Portsmouth, N. H. [George] died at Sacketts Harbor November 20, 1876, leaving four children.

sent to Lowville Academy, Lewis County, State of New York
[Fig. 1]. This place is about [twenty-five] miles from Water-
town. We remained there about two years. I liked the village, which was, and is still, one of the most pleasant ones in
that part of the State. I also liked the school, the principal
was then Mr. Stephen Taylor.[8] I boarded in the family of Dr.
Perry, an excellent man with whose family I became much
attached. While at school here, the boys, every Saturday
used to go to Black River, about two miles distant to bathe
and shoot. The celebrated "John Brown Tract" of land borders the Black River at this point, and the boys often pen-
etrated it for some distance, although we knew it was full
of [11] wild animals. Panthers were killed several times near
where the boys used to go. This is still a vast and untrodden
wilderness. It is so cold that corn and wheat seldom come to
maturity, so that of the many persons who have gone there
to settle and cultivate the soil, none have remained. At the
time I was at school at Lowville, a number of Germans took
up land in the John Brown tract, but they all abandoned it
within two years after their arrival.

In going to Kingston we used to take the stage to Sacketts
Harbor, where we took small sailing schooners for Kingston.
On one occasion when returning home this way to spend my
vacation our vessel was shipwrecked in Reed's Bay near the
extreme end of Wolfe Island in Lake Ontario. The passengers escaped to the shore where we built a fire and remained
two days. There were no houses near. On the morning of the
third day we learned from a man who came to cut wood near
us, where we were. Two of the passengers and myself then
set off, and after a [12] tiresome walk of some ten or twelve
miles through the woods, we came to a settlement opposite

Kingston. Here we took a boat and crossed over, reaching the town towards evening. I went at once to the owners of the vessel, gave them information where the schooner (the Rambler) was, when a vessel with a number of men were sent to the party. It was three days before the remainder reached Kingston.

I think I remained two years at Lowville, after which, I was sent to a boarding school in Montreal, kept by an Irish gentleman named Wm. Ryan. Here I remained a year. In the autumn an incident occurred which I shall never forget. In a garden adjacent to the house where we boarded were some pear trees. Tempted by the fine fruit the boys, myself among the rest, climbed the walls, entered the garden, and brought away a quantity of pears which we stowed away in our trunks. The result was, on my part, a very severe dysentary. I lay at the point of death for several days. It was several weeks before I was able to resume my studies; and not long after this, I returned home.

[13] My father now lived in a new place a mile from Kingston on the river shore, where there was a fine view of the lake. Our house was a handsome brick one, two stories high with wings of one story. Near it was a fine garden and an orchard. I was very fond of working on the place and used

FIGURE 1 (*opposite*). John Russell Bartlett as a student at Lowville Academy in upstate New York. This crayon drawing was done in either 1819 or 1820 when Bartlett was 14 years old. Although sometimes described as a possible self-portrait, there is a note on the back of the original drawing, written in Bartlett's hand, that reads, "Taken while I was a student at Lowville Academy, Lewis County, New York, by a German from whom I took lessons in crayon drawing." Many of the spots or blemishes present on the original drawing have been removed in this reproduction. Courtesy of the John Carter Brown Library.

FIGURE I

to spend my time in transplanting trees, and laying out the grounds. My father employed a gardener and several men. Back of the house and garden the estate extended a mile most of which was under cultivation. I used to enjoy tearing up new land, drawing fallen trees and stumps together, by the aid of a yoke of oxen, and thus making a large fire. Some of the finest trees on the estate were planted by me. I remember once of removing a very live pine tree, which, with the aid of several men, we got on a sled, and then by the aid of oxen, transported to the lawn near my father's house.

When a boy I had a great passion for what are called manly sports, such as shooting, fishing, sailing, ball-playing and skating.

[14] I was never so happy as in a sail-boat, and was familiar with all the bays, islands, shoals and fishing grounds in the St. Lawrence for miles around and near Kingston. Cataraqui Creek I traced on foot with my gun a long distance and knew just the points where the ducks would fly in the proper season; where plover, snipe, partridges and pigeons where [were] to be found. I thought nothing of walking to Collin's Bay, seven miles distant with my gun on my shoulder; sometimes carrying home a few ducks and sometimes having none; but I enjoyed the sport greatly.[9] In the winter I skated a great deal, and long distances on the St. Lawrence. I used to have an ice-boat which I built myself. When there was a stiff breeze I would get eight or ten boys on my boat, and dash off over the glassy ice for five or ten miles at a speed scarcely attained by a locomotive on a railroad. These ice-boats were then common at Kingston, and I believe are still used there. They have recently been introduced on the Hudson river.

[*1824–1836, Rhode Island*]

[15] In employing myself on the farm, I felt that I was not preparing myself for the active duties of life; and as I did not intend to be a farmer I thought I ought to be acquiring a knowledge of business. In the year 1824, being then 18 years of age I left home and came alone to Providence and entered the store of my uncle William Russell [No. 45] Westminster Street, and became an inmate of his family. He then lived on the corner of Star and Benefit Street. My uncle's was the first dry-goods store in Westminster Street, and was directly opposite where the Arcade now stands. Previous to that time all the dry goods business was carried on in Cheapside, North Main Street. I think the only shop besides his in Westminster Street, was the tin shop of Mr. Johnson, father of Capt Johnson of the Navy. Many thought Mr. Russell was hazarding a great deal in trying business in such an out-of-the-way place. Nevertheless the experiment was successful, and the north side of the street from his store to the bridge was soon occupied with shops of various kinds. On the south side were dwelling [16] houses, and it was not until many years later that any one ventured to open a shop on that side of the street.[10]

The Arcade was built while I was a clerk for my uncle. I saw every column raised and most of its stones from the foundation to its completion.[11] When it was finished my uncle removed there and continued the business until a short time before his death in the year 1857 (April 12).

In 1828 I returned to my fathers in Kingston, but had been there only a short time when Mr. Cyrus Butler wrote to me, offering me a place in his Bank, the Bank of North

America. I returned at once and entered upon the duties of bookkeeper; acting also as teller. Mr. John Taylor was Cashier. It was also a part of my duty to open the bank, make the fire and sweep out the office. I then went to Mr. Butler's house, over the bank, got the keys of the vault, took out the money, papers and books preparatory to business. There were then ten banks in Providence, viz. the Providence, Exchange, North America, Eagle, Roger Williams[,] Union, Merchants, Mechanics[,] [17] High Street, and Mechanics & Manufacturers.[12]

During the three years I was in the Bank of North America I saw Mr. Butler every day, and I think no one possessed a better knowledge of his character than I did. He spent much time in the Bank and was always very sociable when there. I always sat with him, by his request when he took up paper offered for discount, and he generally asked my opinion as to the standing of various mercantile houses. When I called for the keys I generally found Mr. Butler at breakfast when he always had a few words to say. I do not think he ever read any thing but the newspapers, and that he possessed no knowledge of the world beyond what he obtained from newspapers. But in all matters of business he showed a remarkable sagacity. While I was with him I do not remember that he met with but a single loss by banking, and in this case he took merchandize in payment, so that, even here he may have recovered the full amount of the debt. He was exceedingly economical in his personal expenses, and I speak [18] within bounds when I state that his personal expenses, including housekeeping did not exceed one thousand dollars a year.[13]

While with Mr. Butler I projected the Athenaeum and successfully carried my plans into effect [Fig. 2]. Nothing could be done without Mr. Butler's aid, as it was to be located in the Arcade of which building he owned the whole of the east side. He was reluctant for some time to take part in the institution, but when it was shown him that it would carry a great many people to the Arcade, and furthermore that he might, if so disposed, sell out his shares, he finally consented and subscribed twelve hundred dollars towards funding the Library & Reading room. Many of the other stockholders in the Arcade subscribed one hundred dollars each, so that a sufficient amount was secured to commence the work. A room was hired in the second story of the Arcade on the west side of the building, and here, in addition to the books, were the leading newspapers including the London Times. Dr. Thomas H. Webb and the Rev. Fred. A. Farley, with whom I was, for many [19] years, on terms of close intimacy, labored with me in establishing the Providence Athenaeum.[14] Dr. Webb and I were on the library committee to purchase the books, and I seldom visited New York without making purchases. I also watched the auction sales very closely and secured some bargains at them. For the first year & it may have been for a longer period I performed the duties of librarian, besides making the first catalogue of the books. Several years after, while living in the city of New York, I raised by subscription the money to purchase the great Description of Egypt published by order of Napoleon I which cost $500. I think there were then but two or three other copies in the country. I also raised the money to buy the Musée Francaise and the Musée Royale. Both of these works I bought in New York.[15] The table or case in which the work on Egypt is kept, the model of an Egyptian temple, was painted by me. The columns were sent to me in New York. The figures and hieroglyphics on this model were all copied from examples found in the work[16] [Fig. 3].

[20] While employed in the Bank of North America I became engaged to Eliza A. the daughter of Christopher Rhodes of Pawtuxet.★

In the spring of 1831 I was chosen cashier of the Globe Bank, a new institution, of which William Sprague, grandfather of the present Governor and Senator William Sprague was the President. He was the founder of the house, and then quite an aged man. At his death his sons Amasa and William continued the business under the firm of A. & W. Sprague.[17] As soon as I entered on my duties as Cashier I was married. This took place on the 15th of May 1831. We were married on a fine day at Pawtuxet, and immediately came [21] to Providence and took possession of our house over the bank at No.

★ Christopher Rhodes had four children, George A. born Mch. 3, 1806, died July 3, 1850. Christopher S. born Aug. 15, 1808, died [Jan. 17, 1861]. Eliza A. born Oct. 28, 1810, died Nov. 11, 1853. Sarah A. Rhodes b. Aug. 14, 1815, d. [July 11, 1854] married Henry B. Anthony. My children are as follows: Elizabeth [Dorrance], born 183 [June 1,1833], died [October 8, 1840]. Anna Russell, born October 19, 1835, married John Antoine Duvillard December 12, 1857. He died at Fort Hamilton, New York May 8, 1865. She died April [13] 1885. Henry Anthony Bartlett, born August 19, 1838 [died August 9, 1901]. George [Francis] born November 26, 1840, died Sept. 8, 1842. John Russell born September 26, 1843 [died November 22, 1904]. Leila, born July 11, 1846, died October 4th, 1850. Fannie Osgood, born April 28, 1850, died in Albany [July 17, 1882].

FIGURE 2

The Providence Athenaeum, of which Bartlett was one of the original pro-
jectors in 1831, has occupied this granite building at 251 Benefit Street
since 1838. Bartlett was one of the original shareholders and officers of
the Athenaeum, remaining active in the affairs of the organization until
his death in 1886. Many of the Athenaeum's most valuable volumes were
obtained through the efforts of Bartlett after he moved to New York City
in 1836. At one time, the Providence Franklin Society, another organization in which Bartlett was a very active member, occupied the lower level
of the Athenaeum's building. Photo by Jerry E. Mueller.

[*blank*] South Main Street.[18] This building has since been
torn down, and the present one erected in its place.

I retained the office of Cashier of the Globe Bank six years,
leading a very quiet and domestic life. My leisure hours were

FIGURE 3

The Egyptian Table and Cabinet at the Providence Athenaeum, ca. 1838, was designed by John Russell Bartlett and painted and decorated by Bartlett and Kingsley C. Gladding. This table was built to house the elephant folios of several important works acquired by the Providence Athenaeum in the 1830s. The hieroglyphs that decorate the sides and columns of the table were personally selected by Bartlett from illustrations in the Athenaeum's volumes on Egypt. At the time the Egyptian Table was constructed, Bartlett had moved to New York City to work as a partner in a commission house, but he maintained his close ties to the Athenaeum and helped obtain some of the organization's most valuable books at sales and auctions. The columns seen in the photo were originally freestanding. They were manufactured in Providence and shipped to Bartlett in New York where the hieroglyphs were applied; once decorated, the columns were returned to Providence for insertion along the two sides of the table.

The Egyptian Table was initially the centerpiece of the reading room on the first floor of the Athenaeum. By the early 1850s, the Athenaeum was renovated to create more space for books; a staircase was added to connect the old reading room with the basement; and the Egyptian Table was moved to the basement level, where it now resides beneath the staircase. No longer used to house the very valuable elephant folios for which devoted to reading and study. I also devoted a portion of my time to painting. Nearly all the pictures now in my house painted by me were the work of my leisure hours while connected with this Bank.[19] We used to see a good deal of young company, in a familiar way, and having a large circle of friends, my house was much resorted to by young [22] people. Sarah Rhodes, my wife's sister passed most of her time with us where she made the acquaintance of Henry B. Anthony whom she afterwards married. Mr. Rhodes came to see us every day and always took dinner with us. On Sundays, when the weather was pleasant, a chaise was sent in for us to take us to Pawtuxet to pass the day. This was our routine of life while I remained in the Bank.[20]

The Franklin Society was then in its palmiest days. William T. Grinnell was its President. The Society embraced most of the scientific men in Providence. It held weekly meetings, at which papers were read. It also had courses of Public Lectures by the members, in which I always took part. The first lecture I ever delivered was before the Franklin Society.[21] I always took a deep interest in this Society and the Athenaeum. I was also a member of the R. I. Historical Society.

About this time the inscription on the Dighton Rock was attracting the attention of antiquaries in Europe. The Royal Society of Antiquaries at [23] Copenhagen, Denmark,

FIG. 3 (*cont.*)

it was constructed, the table today is still used for storage and layout purposes, and as a decorative piece of furniture, it remains an attraction for visitors. Remarkably, the table is still in good condition, save for the scuff marks readily apparent along its base. Photo courtesy of the Providence Athenaeum.

requested the R. Island Historical Society to furnish certain information regarding it. Doct. Webb and myself accordingly (whether by request of the Society I do not remember) went to Dighton, when I took a careful drawing of the rude figures which are engraven on the rock. We transmitted a copy of this drawing to the Society referred to, accompanied by replies from Dr. Webb to the several queries proposed by its Secretary, C. C. Rafn. This correspondence was printed in the large volume called the "Antiquitates Americanae" accompanied by my drawing of the sculptures on the rock. I was made a member of this Society which further honored me with the presentation of a copy of this elegant work on <u>large paper</u>. Professor Rafn in his essay in this book endeavors to prove that the Northmen, in 'their' supposed voyage to Vinland, (which they try to show was what is now Rhode Island) sailed up Taunton river, and, in the sculptures referred to, left a record of their voyage. I fully believe that the Northmen visited the coast of America in the 10th and succeeding [24] centuries as is shown in the ancient Icelandic sagas. (see the English translation in my library) I think these navigations traced our coast down as far as Narragansett Bay which they entered and may have visited afterwards; but there is nothing on the Dighton Rock that in the least resembles the Icelandic runes, or any figures made by this people. I think the rude figures on this rock are the work of the Indians, probably the amusement of their idle moments. I cannot see that there is any intention to record any great event.[22]

My constant confinement while in the Globe Bank impaired my health. I had constant sick head-aches, so severe too, that I was unable to attend to business. I thought a change for some other business, attended with more activity would be more conducive to my health and give me a larger income which I needed for the support of my increasing family. My salary when I first entered on my duties as Cashier was $700, and the use of the upper part [25] of the house. The salary was afterwards increased to a thousand dollars. The largest then paid to any Cashier was $1500, and this was deemed very large.

By the aid of my friends, many of whom took an interest in my welfare, I made an arrangement with the house of Jessup, Swift & Co. Commission Merchants, at 66 Pine Street, New York. I was received into the house as a partner. They had a large monied capital and bank facilities to any amount required. My friends among the manufacturers agreed to send the house all the goods they could sell.

[1836–1849, New York City]

I removed with my family, then consisting of my wife and two children, Elizabeth and Anna, to New York in 1836 and took board in a house in Hudson Street, opposite St. John's Park. Our business went on very well at first, and for nearly a year, or about a year, when a great commercial crisis took place, known as the crisis of 1837. The banks all suspended specie payment, a large number of merchants failed, among them thirteen Domestic Commission houses, embracing [26] that of Jessup, Swift & Co. We compromised with most of our creditors by paying the full amount in goods to all who would accept them—to others a certain amount in cash. But as all our debts could not be paid we were unable to do but little business. The firm was dissolved, when Mr.

Henry Swift and myself continued the business on a limited scale for two or three years, making barely enough for our support.

Soon after I took up my residence in New York I was invited to become a member of the New York Historical Society. This society had not met for years and was almost extinct. It was proposed that a number of gentlemen interested in historical investigations should become members and thereby revive it. It was an old institution, but many of its members were dead, others had left the city and others had become superannuated and ceased to take an interest in the Society. Its collection of books, then small, and its collections of manuscripts were then stowed away in the fourth story of a building on the south-west corner of [27] Broadway and Chambers Street. It was found very difficult to get a meeting of a quorum of the Society or even of its Directors. However a quorum was obtained and a number of persons elected members. The Rev. Dr. Hawks and Mr. George Folsom joined about the same time that I did. We met at this upper room amid the dust and rubbish which had been accumulating for years, and elected Peter G. Stuyvesant, a direct descendant of the celebrated Peter, so celebrated in Irving's Knickerbocker's History of New York. Mr. Stuyvesant was flattered by the honor conferred on him, and soon after becoming the purchaser of a fine granite building on Broadway known as the Stuyvesant Institute, he tendered the Society the use of all the room they wanted for their library and other collections and a hall for their meetings. We now elected large numbers of prominent citizens members, had regular monthly meetings at which papers were read and got up a course of public lectures in the large lecture room of the building, which were well attended and from which the Society [28] derived some pecuniary advantages. Besides this it became better known and began to receive valuable donations of books, newspapers, manuscripts, portraits, etc. I took part in all the proceedings by reading occasional papers and delivering lectures in the course. For many years I was Corresponding Secretary of the Society, as well as a member of the Executive Committee; indeed, I held both those offices until my removal from the city. The Society increased so much that we had neither room for our collections, nor for the members who attended the monthly meetings. In this emergency the New York University which did not use their whole building tendered the society the use of such rooms as they required, free of charge. The offer was accepted and the Society removed to the University building on Washington Square. Here it continued to flourish, by a large increase of members, and by large additions to its library and collections. It has since erected a noble structure on the Third Avenue and maintains the first position among the historical [29] Societies of the country. For several years Mr. Gallatin was its President. His name and reputation as a scholar and a statesman did much for the Society.[23]

In the year 1840 or 1841 Mr. William C. Hall, a dealer in books in London, who had for several years sent large quantities of books to the United States offered to consign to me all his books if I would enter into the book business. As I was not familiar with the business, I proposed to Mr. Charles Welford to join me in it. He did so, when we formed a copartnership under the name of Bartlett and Welford, and took a store in the building adjoining the Astor House under the American Hotel, but soon after removed to a store in the Astor House. We dealt largely in English and Foreign books, for besides the quantities consigned us by Mr. Hall, we imported largely on our own account from England and France. Mr. Welford went personally to London where he made large purchases. B & W were the first to keep a large stock of choice old books in every department of literature, hence our establishment was the resort of literary men [30] not only from New York, but from all parts of the country. FitzGreen Halleck and Fenimore Cooper were <u>daily</u> visitors, and would sometimes remain for hours, generally in conversation. Others would come in and look over the new books. There was scarcely a literary or scientific man in the city who did not pay frequent visits to our store, and the same class of men from other cities generally made us an early call on visiting the city to see what there was new among books. With the clergy of the city and county we had also a large trade.[24]

With the venerable Albert Gallatin I became acquainted about the time I commenced the book business, and as our tastes were much alike for geographical research, antiquities, philology, etc. we became quite intimate. At his request I made him frequent calls, and I may add that for many years previous to his death which took place in 1849 scarcely a week was suffered to pass without passing an evening with him. He was very fond of seeing distinguished strangers, not those however who had become so from mere political [31] preferment, but whose names were distinguished in the fields of science and literature. It was well known in New York that I always had free access to Mr. Gallatin, hence I was frequently applied to by residents of the city as well as by strangers themselves to be introduced to the venerable statesman and scholar. Before taking strangers to him, I invariably sent him a note stating that I would, at a certain hour call upon him with the gentleman named. When the individual I was about to present to him was one with whose literary labors I thought he might not be familiar, I would say that he was the author of such and such books; or, if a traveller, that he had visited such and such parts of the world. He was always glad to see foreign travellers and would astonish them with the knowledge he possessed of the countries they had visited. I remember once to have waited upon him with Captain Graah [Wilhelm A. Graah], a distinguished Danish navigator, who had commanded an expedition for the discovery of the famous lost colony, as it was called in East [32] Greenland. On leaving the house, the Captain told me that he had never met with any one so familiar with the geography of the Arctic regions as Mr. Gallatin, and that he had astonished him with the knowledge he possessed of the history of Denmark, as well as of the north of Europe generally.

In 1842, I suggested to Mr. Gallatin the idea of a new society, the attention of which should be devoted to Geography, Archaeology, Philology and to enquiries generally connected with the human race. This would involve subjects which did not come within the scope of the Historical Society, and hence would not in the least interfere with it. The American Antiquarian Society was quite local, and our enquiries would extend to all parts of the globe, and to all nations. Mr. Gallatin was pleased with my suggestions, and I determined to propose the same thing to other gentlemen. All with whom I spoke, and these were gentlemen who had devoted more or less time to the subjects which we proposed to devote ourselves to, had written books or essays upon these subjects, or had become noted as travellers [33] in foreign countries. These gentlemen accordingly met at my house to exchange views preparatory to an organization. Those present on this occasion were Mr. Gallatin, John L. Stevens [Stephens] the distinguished traveller, Mr. Catherwood [Frederick Catherwood], Rev. Dr. E. Robinson, Rev. Dr. F. L. Hawks, Mr. Charles Welford, Henry R. Schoolcraft, George Folsom, Alexander I. Cotheal, etc. The result was the formation of the American Ethnological Society.[25] Mr. Gallatin was made President.

Other gentlemen prominent in the field of science and letters were afterwards admitted—among those in New York City who took a deep interest in the Society were Messrs. Thomas Ewbank, A. W. Bradford, Theo. Dwight, Jun., Daniel Embury, Prof. W. W. Turner, H. C. Murphy, Elias Loomis and others. The Society had frequent meetings, which were always fully attended. These meetings were held chiefly at the house of Mr. Gallatin or my own; but owing to the infirmities of Mr. Gallatin who was then eighty years of age, he requested that the [34] meetings should be held at his house. The Society cheerfully consented to the wishes of our venerable friend and the meetings afterwards took place at his house. Mr. Gallatin enjoyed these meetings greatly. We assembled early and remained until 11 o'clock. Our President always had a great deal to tell us connected with geographical studies, new voyages and travels or reminiscences of his early life. New books, maps, antiquarian objects, etc. were always laid before the members for discussion. Papers, too, were generally read at these meetings. If any distinguished stranger happened to be in town Mr. Gallatin desired the members to write them to be present at our meetings. Mr. G. always provided an excellent supper. The members at first protested against these suppers as an innovation but as Mr. Gallatin claimed the privilege and could well afford the expense we could say no more.[26]

My venerable and beloved friend died in his 89th year (I think it was). His mind continued sound to the last. At first he became so feeble that he could not leave his room—next he was confined to bed—and even while he lay here [35] his mind seemed active. I visited him every day during the latter part of his life. While he lay in bed he had a slate and pencil with which he amused himself with mathematical and algebraic problems. The finances of the country always had attraction for him—so with banks and banking, and when he could not hold a book in his hand he would amuse himself with questions of finance.

The Annexation of Texas, and the war with Mexico caused Mr. Gallatin much uneasiness.[27] He presided at a great meeting on the subject of the Annexation of Texas, to which he was opposed, and wrote a good deal on both subjects. His essay entitled "Peace with Mexico" coming from a well-known Democrat and friend of Jefferson did more than any thing towards effecting a peace. This essay was written by me at Mr. Gallatin's dictation; or, rather, I should say, I was his amanuensis, for he was so feeble that he wrote with difficulty. I procured such materials as he desired, and aided him in hunting up facts. His essay awakened a deep interest throughout the country, and a large [36] sum of money was contributed chiefly in Boston and New York for printing and distribution some hundreds of thousands of copies of the pamphlet throughout the United States. It was also reproduced in the newspapers and its circulation greatly increased thereby. All the particulars of the publication of this Essay, with the notes, in the handwriting of Mr. Gallatin to me, my replies thereto, a memorandum of the subscriptions & mode of distribution are bound up in a small volume in Green morocco and preserved in my library. On Mr. Gallatin's death, at the request of the New York Historical Society, I read before it, some reminiscences of the distinguished statesman and scholar. See Proceedings of the Society for the year 1848. See also the Transactions of the American Ethnological Soc. for particulars of our meetings, two volumes of which are in my library. Hist. vol. pub. in 1845. At several meetings of the Society I read a continuous paper on the "Progress of Ethnology"* which I afterwards extended and published in a separate volume. I also read an essay [37] on the supposed discovery of America by Madoc. The latter was made the subject of a lecture which I delivered in New York. I enlarged it very much but have never been satisfied with it, or would have printed it. The best reason, however, is that I lent the manuscript to Doctor Hawks, who kept it 12 years, and then only returned one half of it. It has been and still is my intention to rewrite the lost portion and then print it.[28]

It may be proper here to mention an incident connected with the journeys of Mr. John L. Stephens to Yucatan and Central America as I claim to have first suggested them to Mr. S.

No book on travels ever awakened a deeper interest in New York that [than] Mr. Stephen's "Incidents of Travel

* Progress of Ethnology

in Egypt, Arabia Petraea and the Holy Land," published in
1837. Soon after its publication I one day said to Mr. Stephens
when in my office "Why do you not undertake the exploration of Yucatan and Central America? Here is a field," I
added, "that is quite unexplored, where there are numerous objects of interest in ruined cities, temples and other
works of art." [38] Mr. Stephens said he had never heard of
these remains and would be glad to know more about them.
I invited him to come to my house when I would show him
Waldeck's work on Yucatan, a beautiful work in folio, containing views of some of the ruined edifices in that country,
which I had imported a short time previous from Paris.[29] Mr.
Stephens called at once upon me and examined the book. At
the same time I showed him several other books on the countries in question, and pointed out to him in other works,
references to the ancient remains in Yucatan and Central
America. Mr. Stephens was greatly interested in what I
showed him and took some of the books home with him for
a more careful examination of them. He called on me several
times afterwards to talk about the countries in question and
manifested a desire to visit them.

While we were talking these matters over Mr. Leggett
[William Leggett], of New York, our minister in Central
America died, and Mr. Stephens, whose politics were the
same as Mr. Van Buren's, applied to the President (Van
Buren) for the vacant place. [39] He was supported by a large
number of prominent men in New York, and his name, being
at the time, very prominent before the country by his interesting book of travels in the East he was appointed to the
vacant mission. He had several interviews on the proposed
visit to Central America, and Mr. Stephens determined that

as soon as he had presented his credentials and attended to the Diplomatic duties with which he was charged he would undertake the exploration of Yucatan. Fortunately for him, Mr. Frederick Catherwood, a distinguished architect and draughtsman who had spent much time in Egypt and the Holy Land, and with whom he was on intimate terms, was then in New York. Mr. Catherwood had great enthusiasm in every thing appertaining to architecture, and was an ardent lover of the picturesque, and of archaeological researches. Mr. Stephens made him a favorable offer to accompany him to Central America, which offer he at once accepted. They secured such additional aid as they deemed necessary, and in a short time to their departure. [40] Mr. Stephens took all my books relating to the country with him. The result of his journeys is before the world.[30]

While I was engaged in the book business I became acquainted with Mr. E. G. Squier, then living in Columbus, Ohio. Knowing my connection with the Ethnological and Historical Societies in New York Mr. Squier wrote to me giving me an account of his researches among the ancient tumuli and mounds in Ohio.[31] After he had completed his researches he visited New York bringing with him the numerous objects that he and his associate Mr. E. H. Davis had taken from the mounds; also a large number of surveys and drawings of the ancient earth works of the Mississippi valley. Accompanying these were copious notes prepared by him on the subject of these ancient relics and earth works in question. I took Mr. Squier at once up to Mr. Gallatins who manifested the deepest interest in his researches. Mr. G. called the Ethnological Society together, when Mr. Squier exhibited his interesting collection and explained to the society his drawings and surveys, all of which awakened much interest [41] among the members. Mr. Gallatin expressed a desire that the Society should publish what Mr. Squier had collected and written, and, as the Society had no means of its own, agreed to bear the whole cost of publication himself. Mr. Squier at once set to work in New York to prepare the volume for the press. He took a room in the lower part of Broadway where he labored incessantly in putting upon wood-blocks the various drawings of his mound relics.

Previous to this state of Mr. Squier's work, I should say that he went to Washington where he exhibited to Professor Henry [Joseph Henry] of the Smithsonian Institution and to other gentlemen his manuscript and drawings which attracted much attention. The institution was then in its infancy, and its plan of operations had not been matured. Mr. Squier's labours, however, were considered of so much importance, and withal, being so purely American in its subject, that the Board of Trustees expressed a desire to print his work as the first volume of the Smithsonian Contributions to Knowledge. [42] Professor Henry also agreed that if the Ethnological Society would relinquish its claim to print the work that the Smithsonian would print it [in] a superior style in 4to, with all the engravings, maps and plans that Mr. Squier thought proper to add. As the Ethnological Society only desired to see the work printed and made accessible to all, and as it would be executed in a style far superior to that which could be done by it, with the aid of Mr. Gallatin, we all cheerfully withdrew all claim to the work. Mr. Gallatin was also satisfied that it would be better for the Smithsonian Institution, which was a National one, to bring out the book. In due time the work was printed and proved to be the most valuable contribution, by far, that had yet been made to American Archaeology.[32] Indeed, all that had been previously done and written on the ancient tumuli and mounds of the West, if put together would not embrace as many facts as the work of Mr. Squier. It was this work that brought him so prominently before the public, and obtained for him the appointment of United States [43] Minister to Central America, where a wide and comparatively untrodden field for antiquarian research opened itself to him. Mr. Squier's works on Nicaragua and Central America will testify that our government did well in sending him to that country.[33]

In the year 1847 [1848] I published my Dictionary of Americanisms. The beginning of my collections, which collection resulted in this dictionary[,] was made while travelling in a canal boat from Utica, west, on the way to visit my father at Cape Vincent. I amused myself in reading a late work in which the vulgar language of the United States abounded. Being much amused with the strange words and expressions, I marked them on the margin of the book, and on my return to New York noted them down in an interleaved copy of Pickering's Vocabulary. Several books were printed about the same time relating to David Crockett—Stories and adventures in the South-Western States, etc. These I read, noted the particular idioms they contained and afterwards transferred them to my interleaved [44] copy of Pickering. I now became greatly interested in my collection of words, which had so much increased that I had a large blank book prepared into which I transferred all that I had collected. My idea then was to publish a supplement to Pickering's Vocabulary, but I soon found that I had already collected sufficient to make a volume much larger than that of Mr. Pickering. I then came to the conclusion that I would prepare and print a work on an entire different plan, viz. that of a "Dictionary." I now set vigorously to work; ran over the numerous books which contained the familiar and the vulgar or slang language of the country and thus greatly increased my vocabulary of new words with examples of their use. I carried a memo book in my pocket in which I noted down all the new words and phrases that I heard spoken, or read in the newspapers. Then a difficulty occurred as to what were American and what were English in their origin. Many slang words I knew to be American, but there was another [45] class that might with more propriety be styled "Provincialisms" the origin of which I could not determine. In order to learn the history of these I procured from London all the Provincial Glossaries that could be obtained, which I examined from beginning to end, thereby learning which of these words had an English origin. I also procured the most important dictionaries of the English language as Webster, Worcester, Todd's Johnson, Richardson, Knowles, Perry, Sheridan, Ash and many others—also some of [the] earliest that could be found. All these I carefully examined from beginning to end. Of course I examined them but hastily, noticing only the particular classes of words which I proposed to include in my dictionary. When finished the work was published by Bartlett and Welford and met with a ready sale. The edition consisted of but seven hundred and fifty copies.[34]

No other events that I can now think of occurred to me that are worth mentioning while I was engaged in the book business except a series of literary reunions which I gave. The Directors [46] and officers of the N. Y. Historical Society undertook to give these soirees or reunions, but they gave such costly entertainment that they proved a failure; for only the rich could give such, and the gentlemen of limited means refused to attend them. After this failure I proposed a series of reunions to some of the prominent officers and members of the Society at which I pledged myself to give the most simple entertainment as tea, coffee and cake. Mr. Gallatin heartily approved my plan and said he would attend the gatherings. Several other men distinguished in the field of Literature and Science also agreed to honor me with their company. I gave the invitations personally, and explained my plan to each as I invited them. The evening came, and my parlors were filled, some sixty or seventy gentlemen were present. My company expressed much satisfaction with the gatherings and promised to come when ever I might again invite them. Three weeks after I had another—nearly every one whom I had invited was present and the affair passed off very satisfactorily to me, and I believe [47] to all the others. I continued these reunions or soirees two winters, if not more. My rooms were always filled and I never gave my company anything except the articles mentioned. Gentlemen who attended these reunions often asked the privilege of bringing distinguished strangers, who, I was, of course very glad to see. On one evening I remember five clergymen of different denominations were present. At another time the Prussian and French Ministers were present. Baron Roenne [Baron von Roenne] and M. Poussin [Guillaume T. L. Poussin]. The latter was sent from the Republican government then ruling France as a Republic. He spent considerable time in New York, and was a frequent visitor at my house. I shall long remember these reunions as among the most pleasant incidents connected with my twelve years residence in the city of New York—and even now when eighteen years have passed since I left that city, my old friends, when I meet them often mention these gatherings. My friend Thomas Ewbank never meets me without alluding to our meetings, and I will remember how much Baron Roenne was pleased [48] with Mr. Ewbank, particularly when he learned his history. He requested the card of Mr. E—— and a few days after called on him. I lived at No. 1 Amity Place, which was the first house in Laurens [Laurend] Street, south of Amity Street at the time these events took place, and lived there for the last five years that I lived in New York.

[1849–1853, Boundary Commissioner]

In 1849 I dissolved my connexion with Mr. Welford and returned with my family to Providence. The expense of living had then increased so much that the business would not support two families, and we had not sufficient capital to extend it. The business was continued by Mr. Welford.

My family then consisted of my wife, my children Anna, Henry, John, and Leila. We took up our residence with my father-in-law, Gen. Christopher Rhodes until I could find business or some employment.

I had long desired to go abroad and thought if I could get some foreign appointment from the government, it would [be] most agreeable to me, and it would enable me to educate my children [49] in Europe. Before leaving New York I had obtained strong letters to President Taylor [Zachary Taylor] and other prominent men in Washington. Indeed I went to that city a year before when I made some valuable acquaintances, who afterwards rendered me service. I took a letter once from my venerable friend Mr. Gallatin to John C. Calhoun, who received me most kindly, and introduced me to Jefferson Davis who was present. The latter also treated me courteously and invited me to call on him, which I did. I met many of the prominent men then in Congress while in Washington. With Thomas H. Benton I also became acquainted, but forget whether Mr. Gallatin gave me a letter to him or not. I think it must have been from Mr. G——— for I dined with Colonel Benton, and never failed to visit him whenever I visited Washington.

I applied for the Mission to Denmark, and my friends in Washington were confident that I would get it. Mr. John H. Clarke U.S. Senator from Rhode Island exerted himself in my behalf. But at the last moment when all the foreign missions had been given [50] away to certain favorites, Mr. Forward, I think it was, of Pennsylvania who had been most instrumental in carrying that state for Gen. Taylor failed to obtain some prominent office for which he was a candidate. There was nothing then left worth having but the mission to Denmark. This his friends claimed and obtained for him.

About the same time John C. Fremont was in California and was looked upon as one of the heroes of the Mexican war, by whose aid California had been wrested from Mexico. Colonel Fremont had been appointed Commissioner under the treaty of Guadalupe Hidalgo for running the boundary line between the United States and Mexico, to supercede Colonel J. B. Weller, the gentleman first appointed.[35] Colonel Fremont had scarcely received his appointment when he was elected the first Senator from the State of California, in the United States Congress. Aware that the Colonel would

be obliged to resign the office of Commissioner, Mr. John
H. Clarke, then a Senator from Rhode Island telegraphed
to me the fact that the Commissionership would have to be
filled again and [51] asked me if I would accept the place if
appointed. I replied immediately by telegraph that I would
accept it, and by mail replied at length in relation to the
office. Although my life and pursuits had always been of a
sedentary character I always had a great desire for travel,
and particularly for exploring unknown regions. I had, also,
ever felt a deep interest in the Indians and was glad of an
opportunity to be thrown among the wild tribes of the interior. I saw too, that there would be a wide field for new
explorations & that if the government would permit these, I
would prefer the office of Commissioner to that of any other.
I went to Washington soon after receiving Mr. Clarke's letter in order to advance my interests.[36] Among those who
interested themselves in my behalf were Jefferson Davis and
Stephen A. Douglas, then Senators in Congress. A military
officer, one who had served in Mexico, claimed the office on
the ground of his military service and of his acquirements as
an officer. Mr. Davis was opposed to the place being filled by
a military man, as he told me, and for that reason voted for
me. Mr. Douglas was particularly friendly, [52] and although
quite ill when my nomination was taken up by the Senate for
action, he rode to the capital solely to give his vote for me,
and then returned to his chamber. This he stated to me himself. Two votes only were cast against my confirmation &
these were by Jesse D. Bright, of Indiana, and Jer. Clemens
[Jeremiah Clemens], of Alabama. I never saw either of these
gentlemen, but learned afterward that they were pledged to
my military opponent.

Upon my confirmation by the Senate I was directed by the Hon. Thomas Ewing, then Secretary of the Interior, to proceed at once to Washington and organize the commission. I was confirmed in June and according to my orders proceeded to Washington and reported to the Secretary. The papers connected with the commission were placed before me and an office given me. In my conversations with Mr. Ewing I gave him my views as to a thorough exploration of the wide district about to be traversed, in connexion with the survey of the Boundary, which being in accordance with his own views he authorized me to give him [53] a draft for my own instructions. I promptly complied with the Secretary's request, and my instructions were prepared accordingly, not varying in the least from my own draft.

On assuming the duties of my new office, I found hundreds of applications for places in the Boundary Commission which I proceeded to fill, nearly all upon the recommendations of Senators and Members of Congress. Col. John McClellan of the U.S. Topographical Engineers had been appointed by the Government as Chief Engineer; and had promised places to many of his friends, which appointments I made. The most disagreeable duties I ever had to perform were the appointments of officers and assistants for the Commission—nearly all the applicants were strangers to me—and too many were urged on me by their Congressional friends merely to get them away from Washington. While engaged in organizing the commission and preparing the outfit President Taylor died, and Mr. Fillmore [Millard Fillmore], then Vice President succeeded to his place as President. I became acquainted with Mr. Fillmore and received [54] from him much kindness and attention.[37]

My commission bore date June 15, 1850. I labored incessantly during the months of June and July to get the Commission ready for the field. All our wagons and ambulances had to be made—and our whole outfit purchased. We had also to build four iron boats which it was supposed would be required on the Rio Grande and the Gila. These boats were constructed in four pieces each, and intended to be put together when the parties reached the rivers. One of the boats was sent round Cape Horn to San Diego, on the Gulf of California where it would be more convenient to launch it into the Colorado River and thence reach the Gila. Lieutenant I. G. Strain,* of the U.S. Navy was attached to the Commission and had charge of the Boats. The purchase of the tents and camp equipage, saddles, harnesses, arms and ammunition, and the great quantity and variety of articles for a party of more than one hundred men including offi-

* Lieutenant Strain accompanied the Commission as far as San Antonio, when he had a difficult [time] with Col. McClellan growing out of the intemperances of the latter. He became so much disgusted with the habits of McClellan with whom he would have to be associated that he resigned his place in the Commission and returned to Washington, where he preferred charges against McClellan for drunkenness and conduct unbecoming an officer and a gentleman. Upon these charges and the accompanying statements from Army officers in Texas, Colonel McClellan was by orders from the Secretary of the Interior removed from the Commission after it reached El Paso—and returned to Washington. Lieutenant Strain was a young officer of much promise, and I regretted extremely to lose him. He afterwards commanded a party engaged in exploring the Isthmus of Darien, where he endured great hardships from which he died. An account of his explorations was printed in Harper's Magazine.

cers was a severe service. My brother George [George F. Bartlett] was made Commissary, and purchased the provisions in New York. Henry Jacobs was appointed [55] to this department and rendered important service. The Quartermaster, Mr. Myers [James Myer], I sent to Texas to purchase horses and mules and have them ready for us on our arrival at Indianola, on the coast of Texas.[38] On the second of August, 1850 [seven] weeks after I assumed my duties as Commissioner, I despatched the Steamer Galveston to Indianola, laden with the stores, and camp equipage of the commission. Nearly all the officers and men about one hundred in number took passage in the same vessel. I remained to procure some further articles of outfit, but chiefly to make up my accounts for Washington. Lieut. A. W. Whipple one of the Engineers of the Topographical Bureau, remained also for the purpose of securing certain astronomical instruments, not then finished.[39] With 3 or 4 others we embarked in the Steamer Georgia for Havana on the 13th August. At Havana [56] we remained two days, then proceeded to New Orleans where, after two days delay we took passage for Indianola. It was a dangerous season, the last of August to visit Havana and New Orleans. Two officers in consequence of exposing themselves at the latter place were taken with fever and left behind. One of them Mr. Chandler [T. W. Chandler], of Philadelphia followed us a week after, the other never rejoined the party.

I will say no more about the Boundary Commission as the whole history of my connexion with it is contained in my "Personal Narrative of Incidents and Explorations in Texas, New Mexico, California, Sonora," etc. in 2 vols 8vo, New York 1854.[40]

[57] The Government publications relating to the Commission are the following. "Report of the Secretary of the Interior made in compliance with a resolution of the Senate calling for information in relation to the Commission appointed to run and mark the boundary between the United States and Mexico," Cong. Doc. 32d Congress 1st Session, Ex. Doc. No 119, 1852.

Letter to A. H. H. Stuart Sec. of the Interior, in Defence of the Mexican Boundary Line, etc., Senate Doc. No. 6, Special Session 1854.

On the completion of the Survey of the Territory afterwards purchased by the United States from Mexico Major Emory published a work, or rather I should say, the government published a work of Emory's in which is a full account of the scientific results of the Boundary Commission while under my charge.[41]

[58] I returned from the Commission in February 1853, coming by way of New Orleans, thence up the Mississippi to Cincinnati, thence to Buffalo to Albany and Providence. After remaining a couple of days at home, I proceeded to Washington where my presence was required. Mr. Fillmore's presidential term would expire on the fourth of March, and it was of importance that I should get as many of my accounts adjusted as possible. Mr. Pearce [Franklin Pierce] was inaugurated on the 4th of March and within a fortnight I was removed and General Gadsden [James Gadsden], of Texas, appointed in my place.[42] Had I been permitted to remain in Texas with the commission I could have completed the survey, which was the portion of the Rio Grande near its mouth in three months at a trifling expense, while the disbanding of the commission, and its return to Washington, with the

organization of a new one incurred an expense of more than fifty thousand dollars. I remained several weeks in Washington trying, in vain, to get my accounts settled, when I returned to Providence & joined my family.

[59] In June 1853, I went to Cape Vincent with my wife and children and employed the summer and the fall until October in writing out my narrative for the press. D. Appleton Co. agreed to publish my work, they advancing the money therefor and to divide the profits with me. Up to this time I have not received a cent from it. They made a mistake in stereotyping it, which added greatly to its cost.

[1853–1867, Rhode Island]

In October 1853 I returned to Pawtuxet with my family. My beloved wife was not well when she reached her father's house and soon after her illness assumed an alarming form. She died on the 11th November following. Her youngest child Fannie was then three and a half years old. Anna had just completed her education and the whole care of Fannie devolved upon her. My son John was then ten years old. Our good friends Mrs. Jacobs and her family of Cambridgeport, Mass., kindly consented to receive John into their family. They had formerly lived in Pawtuxet. The daughters and my wife were children together, and our families had always been on terms of intimacy. I appreciated their kindness in taking my son, who required the care of those [60] who, like them, knew my children and their mother. My family have always felt a strong attachment to Mrs. Jacobs, her sons and daughters, and I feel sure that we shall continue to entertain this feeling while we live.

For more than a year after my return from Mexico I was occupied with the settlement of my accounts with the government. A portion of this time was spent in writing for the Providence Journal. My residence was with my good brother-in-law Henry B. Anthony, Anna and Fannie being with me.[43] Henry was away at school a portion of the time.[44]

In April 1855 my friends proposed to place me on the ticket for Secretary of State. I hesitated for some time whether I would accept it or not; but as I was out of business and desired employment I consented that my name should be used. If elected, I could, when an opportunity was presented to better my situation accept it. I was elected Secretary, and re-elected annually up to the present time. As a curiosity in elections I will state that on one occasion, that of the election when William Sprague was one candidate, [61] and Seth Padelford the other, and when more votes were polled than ever before in the state, I received every vote. I think about 25,000 votes were polled. I doubt whether such an instance ever occurred before in the United States.[45]

In 1856–57 I set to work vigorously to prepare a new edition of my Dictionary of Americanisms. I had for the previous ten years been gathering materials, and now set to work to arrange them, and to rewrite much of the first edition. I made a contract with Little & Brown to publish the book. They agreed to advance the cost of printing and stereotyping it, and to allow me fifty cents on every copy sold. The money so received to [by] me was to go to my credit towards paying the cost of the book.

When this book was off my hands I began the compilation of a "Bibliography of Rhode Island" or catalogue of Books relating to the State. I hardly knew what to do with this work, as the sale would be limited and it would hardly pay the cost of printing. My friend the Hon. Elisha R. Potter, of Kingston, knew that I was engaged in compiling this catalogue, as he had permitted me to transcribe the titles of all the [62] Books and Pamphlets in his collection relating to the State. One day when he was in my office he saw a portion of the manuscript lying on my desk, which he examined and asked me what I intended doing with it. In replying that I would hardly run the risque of publishing it, he said if I would give it to the State he would submit to the General Assembly a resolution to print it at the expense of the State. Mr. Potter, after examining all the manuscript which I placed in his hands expressed the opinion that the work would be an important one for purposes of legislation, as it was a record of every thing that had been published about the State. I consented to give it to the State, as proposed by Mr. Potter, when a resolution submitted by him authorized the printing of it.[46] Five hundred (500) copies only were printed for the State, and while the type was set I had 150 copies printed on large paper for myself, most of which I gave away. The work was favorable [favorably] received, and in several States gentlemen are engaged in compiling similar Bibliographies. I think Connecticut & Massachusetts.

[63] In [blank] I conceived a plan to collect the portraits of distinguished men of Rhode Island to be placed in Brown University. I thought it a pity that no effort had been made to collect these portraits, and that if it were not done soon, while we knew where reliable portraits existed, it could never be done. In the college there were then only the portraits of Nicholas Brown, the Rev. Dr. Manning [James Manning], the Rev. Dr. Wayland [Francis Wayland], Mr.

Thomas P. Ives and the Rev. Dr. Judson [Adoniram Judson], missionary in Burmah. My plan met the approval not only of the friends of the College but of others who were desirous to collect the memorials of Rhode Island's distinguished sons. I then set myself at work and raised the money that would be required to carry out my plan. All the particulars connected with these portraits will be found in Mr. Guild's [Reuben A. Guild] History of Brown University now preparing for publication. I think this volume will give the names of the subscribers.

A year or two after these portraits were secured, feeling a desire to secure a good portrait of King Charles the 2d who gave Rhode Island its charter, and was [64] thereby identified with our early Colonial history, I wrote to my friend Mr. Ethelbert R. Billings, of Providence, then in London, proposing to him to procure a good portrait of Charles, or rather a copy of one. Mr. Billings felt a deep interest in the matter suggested to him and immediately replied to my letter, saying that he had heard of an original portrait of the King, as well as one of his Queen, the Dutchess of Braganza, which he was in treaty for. He subsequently became the purchaser of both these fine pictures which he presented to Brown University.[47] They are now in the gallery in their original frames, which were reguilded and repaired in Providence, and are two of the most valuable portraits in the collection. Mr. Guild's History of the College, before referred to, will doubtless contain fuller particulars, with correspondence, relating to the portraits.

There is another portrait in the College collection, that of General Burnside [Ambrose Burnside], which I collected the money for and had painted by Mr. E. Leutze.[48] When I went to New York to procure a artist to paint this portrait, all connoisseurs agreed that Leutze or Elliott [probably Charles L. Elliott] [65] were the ones to entrust it to. I did not call on Mr. Elliott, learning that he was full of work, and could not paint the picture for some time. It was necessary to do the work at once, while General Burnside was occupied in New York. Mr. Leutze knew the General well, and agreed to set about the work, at once, and finish it as soon as possible. The order, therefore, was given him. I presume that in the history which Mr. Guild has in press the particulars of my connexion with the portraits mentioned will be stated.[49]

On the 10th November 1863, I was married by the Rev. Dr. Bellows at the house of Mr. Benjamin G. Arnold, New York, to Miss Ellen E. Eddy, daughter of Nelson S. Eddy of Providence.[50] We boarded for a while at No. 8 Angell Street, when I bought the dwelling house, now No. 225 Benefit Street, where we removed in the spring of 1865 [and] where we now reside [*both addresses are in Providence*].[51]

When the late rebellion broke out I commenced the collection of slips from the newspapers relating to it. I thought the war might last about a year; nevertheless, having begun the work, I continued it, scarcely omitting a day without clipping & pasting. I think that I labored, on an average three hours [66] a day for four years. I took regularly through the whole war the New York Tribune and the Evening Post Daily. The Times, and the Herald, I took but a portion of the time. From all those my selections were made.[52] I also took considerable from the Providence Journal and other papers. At the same time I collected all the pamphlets and books appertaining to the war that I could lay my hands on, all of which are in my possession. I shall continue to add to it all that appears on the subject of the rebellion, both Books and Pamphlets.[53]

My collection finally increased so much that towards the end of the war, I found that a catalogue was necessary, in order that I might know what I had. I therefore, with much labor made a catalogue. When it was completed, I thought it would be better for me to include in it every thing that had been published relating to the war, whether I owned it or not. I accordingly carried out this plan, and furthermore included in it the titles of all publications appertaining to American Slavery. This seemed properly to belong to [67] the subject, as it was the cause of the war, while emancipation was its result. Then in order that others might derive benefit from my labors, I published the catalogue under the title of "The Literature of the Rebellion," etc.

During the war I also compiled a volume under the title of "Memoirs of Rhode Island Officers who rendered distinguished service to their country in the war of the Rebellion," etc. This was the work of accident.

About a year after the war began and when Rhode Island had begun to be conspicuous through her Generals and other officers, I received frequent applications from publishers of books and newspapers for sketches of Gov. Sprague, Gen. Burnside, Rodman [Isaac P. Rodman], Arnold [Richard Arnold], and of several officers of a lower grade who fell in battle. Of Gov. Sprague I furnished five different sketches. This was a severe tax on my time and the labor brought no remuneration. It then first occurred to me that I would prepare similar sketches to those I had furnished others, but more in detail of all the Rhode Island officers who had been killed and of the commanders from the Major Generals to the Colonels commanding. I advised with my military [68] friends and with other gentlemen in relation to it. They all approved my plan and advised me to go on with it. I did not wish to write a history of the war, but to write a small volume to sell at a low price. My desire was to produce an elegant work with portraits of the officers mentioned. On making my estimate I found that the cost would be so great & the sale so limited that unless a considerable portion of the cost of engraving the portraits could be paid for, I could not realize the cost of the work. Several gentlemen therefore pledged themselves to contribute various sums towards this expense, while others agreed to pay the cost of certain portraits. With this aid I went on with the work, and extended it, so as to include in it sketches of the several Batteries.[54]

[69] The following is a list of my several publications in the order in which they appeared.[55] [*Note Bartlett's double entry for number 13.*]

1. Progress of Ethnology. An account of recent Archaeological, Philological and Geographical Researches in various parts of the Globe tending to elucidate the Physical History of Man. N.Y., Bartlett & Welford, 1847, [151 pp.].[56]

2. Dictionary of Americanisms: a Glossary of Words and Phrases usually regarded as peculiar to the United States. 8vo pp. [412] New York, Bartlett and Welford, 1847 [*should read 1848*].

FIGURE 4 (*opposite*). Oil painting of John Russell Bartlett, ca. 1830, by an unknown artist. This painting is sometimes attributed to Thomas Sully, but there is a strong likelihood that the artist is Bartlett's long-time friend, Henry Cheever Pratt, a noted portrait and landscape artist

FIGURE 4

FIGURE 4 (*cont.*)

who lived in Providence in the 1820s. According to Gray Sweeny, Pratt's "Catalogue of Portraits done at Providence, R. I. 1830," lists a painting of "Mr. John R. Bartlett" that carried a price of $15.00 (see *Drawing the Borderline: Artist-Explorers of the U.S.-Mexico Boundary Survey*, the Albuquerque Museum, 1996, p. 29). The portrait listed by Pratt is likely a copy of one he did for Bartlett, or else Bartlett had not yet paid for the original painting. Either way, the relatively low price of the Pratt painting is consistent with the relatively small size of the Bartlett portrait, and given that Bartlett was a clerk at the Bank of North America and single at the time, there would have been little reason for him to commission a larger portrait from Pratt. The Bartlett portrait is reproduced here by permission of its owner, the Providence Athenaeum.

FIGURE 5

Black paper cutout of John Russell Bartlett, dated 1835, by William Henry Brown, a nineteenth-century artist known for his quality productions of dim figures and silhouettes. In the case of Bartlett, the figure is isolated from his surroundings, whereas in most of the silhouettes by Brown, the central figure is placed in the context of an overall larger scene, most often a room. This suggests the figure of Bartlett reproduced here might have been removed or copied from a larger drawing by Brown. As an adult, and at a height of approximately five feet seven inches, Bartlett was known for his slight build, and this silhouette of him reinforces that physical description. The label on this drawing reads, "Taken while I was cashier at the Globe Bank in 1835. The artist had rooms over the Post Office then in South Main, a few doors below College Hill St. A large no. __ were made of prominent citizens." Courtesy of the Rhode Island Historical Society.

JOHN R. BARTLETT

FIGURE 5

FIGURE 6

John Russell Bartlett, a pencil sketch by Augustus de Vaudricourt, dated and signed by the artist at El Paso, December
1850. Bartlett at this time was the U.S. Commissioner on the
Mexican Boundary Survey, a position he held for nearly three
years. Because photography was still in its infancy and quite
unreliable, Bartlett chose instead to operate in the field with
an artist attached to the Commission, a position initially filled
by Vaudricourt. Shortly after this sketch was made, difficulties with Vaudricourt compelled Bartlett to terminate his
association with the artist, and Vaudricourt would eventually be replaced on the Commission by Henry Cheever Pratt,
a Boston artist. Bartlett added a statement to the bottom of
this sketch that reads, "J. R. B. while on the Boundary Commission," and below that he added a date of "1851." That date
is impossible because Bartlett spent all of December 1851 in
far western Mexico. The original sketch, catalogued as "MS
Amer 1850" by the John Carter Brown Library, has significant condition problems, and the version of the sketch reproduced here has had major restoration work. Bartlett's hair,
receding in the front and worn long on the sides, looks much
the same on most portraits of him from 1850 onwards.

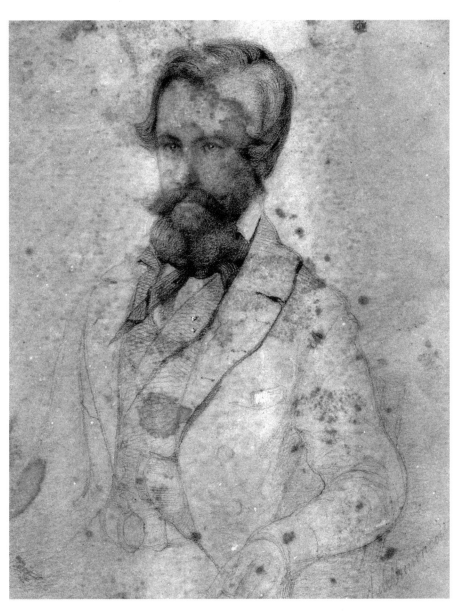

FIGURE 6

John Russell Bartlett at El Paso, October 1852, an oil painting by Henry Cheever Pratt. This painting was done just prior to Bartlett's departure from El Paso for the lower Rio Grande and his eventual return to Providence. Pratt at the time was finishing a series of portraits for prominent local citizens of El Paso, including traders and merchants, James Wiley Magoffin and Benjamin Franklin Coons. It is not known who commissioned this painting, Bartlett or Magoffin, but James Magoffin and his descendants in El Paso owned the painting for many years. Today, there is a copy of this painting at the Magoffin Home State Historical Park in El Paso, Texas, and the original is owned by the Amon Carter Museum of Fort Worth, Texas, which granted permission to reproduce the painting here. Bartlett's hair, unusually long and neatly combed in this portrait, successfully hides the receding hairline that is evident in the sketch of 1850 shown in Figure 6.

FIGURE 7

FIGURE 8

John Russell Bartlett, mechanical print of an undated gelatin photograph. This photograph carries the title, "John Russell Bartlett (1805–1886) as a young man," although it can be argued Bartlett appears as anything but a "young man." In comparing this photograph of Bartlett to an 1852 oil portrait of him by Henry Cheever Pratt (Figure 7), it is clear that Bartlett's hair has receded much further; his beard is considerably less full; and both are much grayer on the photo than on the painting. However, Bartlett's age, based on hair and facial lines, seems greater on an 1859 oil painting of him (Figure 10) than on this photograph. These lines of evidence suggest a date for the photo of after 1852 but before 1859. Perhaps the date of this photo coincides with the year Bartlett became Secretary of State (1855), thus making him fifty years old. Courtesy of the Rhode Island Historical Society. Rhi x3 539.

FIGURE 8

FIGURE 9

A few months after the caption was written for Figure 8, this oil portrait of John Russell Bartlett surfaced. The painting is by James Sullivan Lincoln of Providence, a long-time acquaintance and friend of Bartlett and a noted nineteenth-century portrait artist. Among the Lincoln papers (MSS 537) held by the Rhode Island Historical Society Library is a *List of Portraits Painted by J. S. Lincoln Since A.D. 1837, Providence, R. I.* For July 1857, Lincoln notes he made a copy of Bartlett from a daguerreotype. That daguerreotype is likely the photograph shown in Figure 8. This would explain why the image of Bartlett in this painting is laterally reversed (a mirror image), a common problem introduced by the early daguerreotypes of the 1850s. The painting is signed on the verso, "J. S. Lincoln 1st." Lincoln also indicates he made a copy for Mr. Isaac Brown, another likely acquaintance of Bartlett from among the intellectual societies and organizations of Providence. The portrait presented here is a much-restored copy of the original. It is reproduced here through the generosity of its owner. Private Collection.

FIGURE 9

FIGURE 10

According to the Rhode Island Historical Society, this portrait of John Russell Bartlett was painted by James Sullivan
Lincoln in 1859. However, there is no such entry for 1859 in
the artist's logbook of portraits (MSS 537–James Sullivan Lincoln Papers, RIHS Library). Most striking in this portrait
are: the distance between the subject and the artist; the formal attire of Bartlett; and the rather passive expression on
Bartlett's face. What the artist has captured is the essence of
Bartlett's character: a serious, dedicated, independent, and
somewhat aloof intellectual and gentleman to whom formality
and protocol were very important. In describing this portrait
of Bartlett and another of the poet, William Jewett Pabodie,
C. L. Bert and L. J. McElroy state, "It is fitting that Lincoln's
portraits of Pabodie and Bartlett show the rumpled visages
of men guided by inner vision rather than conventional staid
reality" (in "James Sullivan Lincoln [1811–1888] Exhibit Catalogue," *Sketches*, Number Three, April 1992). Courtesy of the
Rhode Island Historical Society. RHi x3 7712.

FIGURE 10

FIGURE II

3. same. 2nd edition 1859, 3rd Ed. 1861, 4th ed. greatly enlarged. Boston, Little, Brown & Co., pp. 813, 1877. [2nd edition, 524 pp., 3rd edition 524 pp., 4th edition, 813 pp.]

4. Reminiscences of Albert Gallatin. A paper read before the New York Historical Society, December 1849. [NYHS Proceedings, pp. 281–297]

5. Personal Narrative of Explorations and Incidents in Texas, New Mexico, California, Sonora, and Chihuahua, connected with the United States and Mexican Boundary Commission during the years 1850–51–52 and 1853. 2 vols. 8vo, New York, D. Appleton & Co. 1853. [*The correct publication date is 1854.*]

6. Official Despatches and Correspondence connected with the United States and Mexican Boundary Commission. Senate Doc. No. 119, 32nd Congress, 1st Session, 1853.

[70] 7. Letter to Alexander H. H. Stuart, in defence of the Mexican Boundary, with other official Documents. Senate Doc. No. 6, Extra Session.

8. Records of the Colony of Rhode Island and Providence Plantations in New England. Printed by order of the General Assembly. 1636 to 1792, 10 vols., 8vo, Providence, various publishers from 1855 to 1865.

FIGURE 11 (*opposite*). John Russell Bartlett, a photograph taken by Frank Rowell, Providence, Rhode Island, ca. 1861–1862. If the date is correct, Bartlett at this time would have been 56 or 57 years old. Also, he was not only serving as Secretary of State, but likely as Acting Governor as well, for the regular governor, William Sprague, was serving in the Civil War. Relative to the other photographs and portraits of Bartlett from this period, the date of the photograph might be in error, as Bartlett appears to be older than his middle to late 50's. Courtesy of the John Carter Brown Library.

Fifty copies of this work were printed on large paper, at my own expense of paper. A list of the subscribers is in my own copy.

9. A History of the Destruction of His Britannic Majesty's Schooner Gaspee, in Narragansett Bay, on the 10th June 1772; accompanied by the correspondence connected therewith; the action of the General Assembly of the Colony of Rhode Island thereon, and the official journal of the Proceedings of the Commission of Enquiry appointed by King George the Third, on the same. 8vo, Providence, 1862 [*should read 1861*] [Providence, A. C. Greene, 140 pp.].[57]
Printed in the Colonial Records, Vol. VII. 100 copies printed for the General Assembly, in 8vo separately and 125 copies on large paper for J. R. B.

[71] 10. Index to the Printed Acts and Resolves of, and of the Petitions and Reports to the General Assembly of the State of Rhode Island and Providence Plantations from the year 1850 to 1862. Printed by order of the General Assembly. Providence, Alfred Anthony, 1863, xxxiv and 104 pp.

11. Index. The same title. From the year 1758 to 1850. Printed by order of the General Assembly. Providence, Knowles, Anthony & Co., 1856, xliii & 424 pp.
The latter with its full title should precede the former, being the first work; the latter the continuation.

12. Bibliography of Rhode Island. A Catalogue of Books and other publications relating to the State of Rhode Island; with notes Historical, Biographical and Critical. Providence, Alfred Anthony, 1864, iv and 287 pp.

400 copies printed for the State in 8vo and 150 copies for J. R. B. on large paper, royal 8vo.

13. The Literature of the Rebellion. A Catalogue of Books and Pamphlets relating to the Civil War in the United States and on subjects growing out of that event. Together with works on American Slavery, and Essays from Reviews and Magazines, on the same subject. Boston, Draper & Halliday. Providence, S. S. Rider & Co 4to 1866, iv and 477 pp.

[72] Of this work 250 copies were printed in royal 8vo, and 80 copies in 4to.[58]

13. Bibliotheca Americana. A Catalogue of Books relating to North and South America in the Library of John Carter Brown, of Providence R.I.[59]

Part 1.—1493 to 1600. Part 2. 1601 to 1700. With Notes. Providence 1865–1866. 2 vols. royal 8vo.

Only 50 copies of this work were printed, and these exclusively for presents. They have been given to the following persons, viz.

1. James Lenox N.Y.

2. Henry C. Murphy Brooklyn

3. J. Carson Brevoort "

4. Dr. E. B. O'Callaghan N.Y.

5. Col. Rush C. Hawkins "

6. New York Hist. Soc. "

7. State Library of N.Y. Albany

8. Am. Antiquarian Soc. Worcester

9. Public Library Boston

10. Charles Deane "

11. Mass. Hist. Soc. "

12. N. Engld Genealogical Soc. "

13. Brown University Providence

14. Harvard College Liby. Cambridge

15. British Museum London
16. Bodleian Library Oxford
17. Henry Cuth London
18. [*blank*] Scotland
19. Duke of Devonshire Chatsworth, Eng.

20. Royal Library Hague, Holland
21. Royal Library Brussels
22. Imperial Library Berlin
23. Bib. National Paris
24. Henry Stevens London

[73] 14. Memoirs of Rhode Island officers who were engaged in the service of their country during the great rebellion of the South. Illustrated with 34 portraits. Providence, Sidney S. Rider & Bro., 1867. pp. viii and 452.[60]
Of this work 600 copies were printed in quarto, and thirty-five in folio.

15. Dutch translation of Dictionary of Americanisms, "Woordenboek van Americanismen," een lijst van woorden en zinnen, etc. Bewerkt door M. Keijzer, Gorinchem, J. Noorduyn en Zoon 1854 4to [96 pp.]. [*A German translation by Frederich Köhler, under the title of "Wörterbuch der Americanismen," was published in Leipzig in 1866.*]

16. Primeval Man and his Associates. A paper or report read to the American Antiquarian Society at Boston April [29] 1868. Repeated before the New York Historical, and the American Ethnological Societies, the R.I. Historical Soc., The Franklin Society, Providence, and the Friday Evening Club. Printed in the memoirs of the Antiquarian Soc. and 50 copies printed separately [by Tyler & Seagrave, Worcester, 31 pp.].[61]

17. Should come in as No. 8. Letter to Levi S. Chatfield, President of the Atlantic and Pacific Railroad Co. on the practicality of a railroad to the Pacific via El Paso. N. York 1853 (written in reply to a letter from Mr. Chatfield).

18. History of the Wanton Family of Newport R.I. S. S. Rider, Providence 1878 [152 pp.].[62]

[74] No. 19 (Russell Genealogy). Genealogy of that branch of the Russell family which comprises the Descendants of John Russell of Woburn, Massachusetts [1640–1878]. 1879 [Providence Press Co., 212 pp.].

" 20. Letters of Roger Williams 1632–1682. Edited by J. R. B. [Providence: Narragansett Club, 1st series, vol. 6, 1874, 420 pp.].

" 21. The Naval History of Rhode Island. Printed in the Providence Journal 18– [1860–1861] number [*blank*].[63]

[*The following four items are missing from Bartlett's list. It is very likely that entry number 24 was a deliberate omission, given the controversial nature of the subject matter at that time.*]

[22. Census of the inhabitants of the Colony of Rhode Island and Providence Plantations. Providence, Knowles, Anthony & Co., 1858, vol. 238, 120 pp.]

[23. Charter and by-laws of the Sopori Land and Mining Company, incorporated by the State of Rhode Island, June 1859: with a statement, giving the particulars of the estates of the company, and of the mineral regions in the territory of Arizona. Providence, Knowles, Anthony & Co., 1859, 26 pp.] [64]

[24. The barbarities of the Rebels: as shown in their cruelty to the Federal wounded and prisoners, in their outrages upon Union men, in the murder of Negroes, and in their unmanly conduct throughout the rebellion. Privately printed by Bartlett in 1863 under the pseudonym of Colonel Percy Howard, 40 pp.]

[25. The Soldiers' National Cemetery at Gettysburg; with the proceedings at its consecration, at the laying of the corner-stone of the monument, and at its dedication. Printed by the Providence Press Company for the Board of Commissioners of the Soldiers' National Cemetery, 1874, 109 pp.]

[*The next section of the autobiography appears to have been written in 1871 or early 1872, after the establishment of the Third Republic of France, but before Bartlett's second trip to Europe in June 1872.*]

[*1867, First European Trip*]

[75] Recollections of my visit to Europe in 1867.

On the [*blank*] June 1867 I visited Europe. I had wanted for years to go abroad, but my official duties as Secretary of State rendered it inconvenient. At this time, however, an opportunity presented itself which I gladly availed myself of. The State House was to be enlarged and during the progress of enlargement, my office was to be converted into a store-room and rendered inhabitable for several months; so that it would be necessary for me to attend to the duties appertaining to my office at my own house.[65] Then Mr. Desmond FitzGerald who had been my assistant, with the office of Deputy Secretary for nearly four years, was fully competent to attend to any duties that might be required of him; and as he intended to leave me at the close of the year, I could not look forward to the time when I could leave as well as that referred to.

I returned from Newport, where I had been to attend the session of the General Assembly on Saturday and on the fol-

lowing [*blank*] left for New York, embarked on board the
Steamer Bellona for London and Brest, on the [*blank*].

We reached Brest after a passage of fifteen days. The ship
was a slow one and deeply laden. I remained at Brest until
noon of the second day, which gave me an opportunity [76]
to look about the place. It happened to be a fete day, which
brought to the city a large number of the Breton peasantry
from the adjoining villages. The streets were filled with
these people, all of whom were clad in their holiday attire,
which is only worn on similar occasions. These Bretons
are the descendents of the old Celtic stock, and still speak
the Breton language, which is closely allied with the Welsh
and other Celtic dialects of Great Britain and Ireland; and
so general is the use of this language in the North-western
provinces of France, that thousands of these people know
no other, not even the French. The people of each village,
or "clan" if it may be so called, wear a costume peculiar to
themselves, which marks them wherever seen. These costumes are very fantastic and some of them pretty. I bought
at one of the shops a little volume containing color plates of
all the costumes of the district.

Brest being the chief naval depot of France (unless Cher-
bourg may now take the precedency) is strongly fortified. I
walked outside the city among the fortifications some portions of which seemed very old, yet, all are kept in good condition. A sentry stopped me and ordered me away, saying
that no one was permitted there.

A creek or small stream divides the town into two parts
[77] which are joined by a very elegant and lofty iron bridge
of recent construction, said to have the largest swing in the
world. It is 65 feet above the water, with a space of 347 feet

between the piers. The draw opens by machinery to allow ships of war to pass into a basin in the interior, where they are so completely shut in by the high ridges on both sides, upon which the town is built, that only the upper part of the masts are visible. The mouth of the creek may be closed with a boom. It is said that from 30 to 40 men of war may lie within the creek above the bridge. Brest is celebrated as the place where Mary Queen of Scots, when a child, landed in 1548; and a few days afterwards at St. Germain she was affianced to the Dauphin Francis 2d.

We reached Paris at 5 o'clock on the morning of the day following our departure, and put up first at the Hotel du Louvre, Rue Rivoli, directly opposite the Louvre; but a day or two after removed to the Hotel Cher de Rohan, near the Palais Royale. The Great International Exposition was at that time open in Paris, and the city thronged with strangers. I made many visits there, sometimes remaining the entire day, so much was there to be seen. At every visit I found something new, or that I had not discovered before. These visits were excessively fatiguing, so much so, that I found myself unfit for any thing in the evening, and usually returned before nine o'clock.

[78] One day while lounging in one of the picture galleries I met Mrs. Cornelia Greene and her daughter Miss Fanny of Providence. They had been more than a year in Europe, travelling with Mr. Henry Rogers. On another day at the Exposition I saw the Turkish Sultan, and subsequently the Viceroy of Egypt. Seeing a general rush through the avenues, I knew some high dignitary was approaching, and accordingly took my stand near an iron column, where I should escape the rush of the crowd and still see those who

were passing. Soon came a few of the Police; then a party of Turks all dressed in European costume, black frock coats etc., but wearing the universal fez. In the group walked the Sultan, a French officer at his side pointing out objects of interest. The Sultan was dressed precisely like his companions. One day I was presented with tickets of admission to the Turkish Café, an elegant building erected at the expense of the Viceroy of Egypt, where every thing was in Oriental style. Upon entering a Turk conducted me to a divan, and soon after brought me a cup of delicious coffee, followed by a chibouque or Turkish pipe. I threw myself on the lounge and took a few whiffs through the pipe, and found it a great luxury.

At almost every visit to the exposition, I stopped at the mechanical department where Mr. Corliss's famous steam engine was [79] that subsequently took the gold medal. It was always surrounded by admiring spectators, for in its beauty and excellence of workmanship it quite surpassed every other engine of its kind.[66]

I was so fortunate as to find in Paris my old friend and partner Mr. Charles Welford, of New York, who being familiar with the city, accompanied me to every place of interest. One day we rode out to the Bois de Boulogne, and were shown the spot where, a few days before, the Emperor of Russia was fired at by a man in the crowd. The would-be assassin was at once arrested and in course of time was tried, condemned and executed. I also visited the famous cathedral of Notre Dame, St. [blank], the Pantheon, La Madeleine, the church of San Rogue, Hotel Chuny, the Bibliotheque Imperial, now Bib. Nationale, the St. Genevieve Library.

One day I devoted to Versailles, accompanied by Mr.

Welford. We traversed the numerous picture galleries and halls of this magnificent structure, and afterwards walked through the spacious grounds, stopping at the Trianon and Fountains, returning to the palace pretty well fagged out with our long tramp. My friend Col. C. B. Norton procured a ticket for me to visit the catacombs, but friends advised me not to venture there, as they were cold and damp, and that I should run a great risque of taking cold.

[80] Met my friends Mr. E. G. Squier and Frank Leslie many times. Their apartments were in Rue Richlieu not far from my quarters so that I often went there. Mr. Caleb F. Harris and his wife and Miss Harris, his niece, of Providence, were also in Paris while I was there; we often met and took drives and walks together. They had apartments at the Hotel Bristol in Place Verdune. Often in calling there I stopped to look at the beautiful column which was thrown down by the communists a few years after.

The Prince of Wales was at the Hotel Bristol at one time when I was calling on Mr. Harris. I once saw the young man with his companion, who, I supposed was the Duke of St. Albans, step into his carriage and drive off.

While here the International Congress of Archaeology met; and having been appointed a Delegate by the American Antiquarian Society, and the American Ethnological Society, I attended their meetings, which were held in the [*blank*]. The prominent topics before the congress related to Pre-historic times, upon which several papers were read. One day the members were invited to make an excursion to St. Germain, where there is a fine museum of pre-historic remains, and of antiquities belonging to the time of the ancient Gauls. The collection of pre-historic antiquities and animal remains is a national one. The articles, though not numerous, are generally fine specimens; and as the [81] government is making an effort to enlarge the collection, it will doubtless, ere long, be one of the best collections on the continent. The museum occupies the old Royal Palace, which has been renovated and put in fine condition. The decorations of the Gaulic department are all characteristic of the people and the period to which they refer. We were invited to partake of a breakfast about 11 o'clock. About one hundred took their seats at the table, but so miserable were the things spread before us that Mr. Squier, Mr. Blackman myself and others could not stand it, and withdrew to a restaurant near by, where we found something better to our taste. The only meats we had were boiled hog's heads, of which there were several on the table. As this was an article which I had never tasted I declined taking any, and called for beef steak, mutton chop or poultry; but was told there were neither to be had. Even an egg could not be furnished. We came to the conclusion that some restaurant keeper had contracted to entertain the party at a stipulated price for each, and had given us the cheapest possible articles that the market furnished.

I met few dignitaries or men of prominence while in Paris, although nearly all the crowned heads of Europe had been there shortly before my visit, including the Emperor of Russia; Queen Victoria, the King of Prussia, the Emperor of Austria, and Victor Emanuel, King of Italy. The Sultan and the Viceroy of Egypt [82] were the only sovereigns who were there at the time I was. Arrangements had been made for a grand dinner and evening entertainment at the Hotel de Ville for the Sultan; but the day before it was to take place came the news of the shooting of the Emperor Maximilian in Mexico. He was brother to Joseph the Emperor of Austria, in consequence of which all the courts of Europe went into mourning and the dinner was given up. Mr. Thayer, one of the Emperors Council, or a Senator, I don't remember which, to whom I had a letter of introduction, took me in his carriage to see the preparations, which, he said, were on a grander scale than those for Queen Victoria or the Emperor of Russia, both of whom had been entertained there.

Orders had been given for no one to be admitted to the building. On reaching the entrance Mr. Thayer enquired of the guard if any one had been there; the officer in charge said that no one had been admitted except the Mayor and his family. The Sultan had also been there with some of the government officials. "So" said Mr. Thayer, "you will see what none of the people of Paris have seen, or will see, as tomorrow every thing will be removed and the decorations taken down."

An addition of wood had been hastily constructed along one side of the Hotel de Ville, in the same style as the original edifice, and painted so near like it, that one would take it for [83] the original structure. In this addition was the grand dining hall. The table was already set, with all its ornaments of gold, silver and bronze, together with its Sevres porcelain. The chairs were also in their places, and the exact chair which every guest was to occupy was designated. Indeed every thing was there except the eatables, the liquors and the guests. To prepare the Hotel, all the public offices had been closed and vacated by the city officials. A few soldiers, with those who were to wait upon the guests were the only people to be seen in the building. Mr. Thayer did me the honor to say that had the entertainment taken place, he would have presented me a ticket for the evening reception.

This Mr. Ainede Thayer was a Rhode Islander. His father, who was a native of Providence, was in Paris at the time of the old French Revolution of 1798, where he amassed a fortune by purchasing confiscated estates. The son married a daughter of General Bertrand, one of Napoleon 1st's confidential officers.

Mr. Thayer was first cousin to Mrs. Patrick Brown of Providence, the mother of Mrs. John Carter Brown. On presenting the letter to Mr. Thayer, he received me very kindly and offered his services to render my stay agreeable while in Paris. He regretted that he could not entertain me at his house as his wife was very sick; indeed, while conversing with Mr. T. [84] a priest passed through the parlor to Mrs. Thayer's chamber. She died a few weeks after, and Mr. Thayer, himself, who complained of being ill when I saw him, did not long survive his wife. I should observe that Mr. Thayer was a direct descendant of Roger Williams, and that all his relatives lived in Rhode Island, yet he had never visited America. He was fully posted up in the history of his family and seemed to take pleasure in talking of his distinguished ancestor. He knew by name his near relatives in Providence and made enquiry about each of them.

One day when dining with Mr. Squier I met several gentlemen of prominence. Among them I remember Mr. Pascal de Guangos [Pascual de Gayangos] a distinguished Spanish historian who is often mentioned by Prescott [William Prescott] and Ticknor [George Ticknor]. Of the latter he was a particular friend and rendered him much aid in collecting his grand collection of Spanish and Portuguese books, unequalled in the United States and now in the Boston Public Library. Mr. Guayangos [Gayangos] spoke English fluently. I also met on the same occasion Mr. Franks [Augustus W. Franks], of London, a distinguished antiquary and especially learned in pre-historic researches. With Mr. William Blackmore, of London, I also became acquainted here.

A few days after I attended a dinner party given by Mr. Blackmore, at his hotel; some ten or twelve gentlemen were present. Señor Guayangos [Gayangos], Mr. Franks & Mr. Squier [85] were among the guests. I here became acquainted with Mrs. Blackmore, a most estimated lady, who [whose] kindness to me during a dangerous illness in London I shall never forget. Shortly after this, I met Mr. & Mrs. Blackmore and a number of other ladies and gentlemen at some place (I cannot now recollect where) in Paris, to witness the unrolling of an Egyptian mummy. About twenty persons were present. The mummy proved to be that of an Egyptian priest whose name and office was borne upon an inner envelope. The name of the king in whose reign he lived was also stated. The gentleman who did the unrolling seemed familiar with Egyptian antiquities and said that the priest lived in the seventh century before the Christian era. I brought away a long piece of one of the bandages of linen cloth, about three inches in width, which was wound around the body.

The office of Mr. Charles B. Norton was a place of frequent resort for me while in Paris. There I found files of American newspapers and met many Americans. Mr. S. F. B. Morse, of the electric telegraph, was a daily visitor there. I also met here several times Mr. Jacob Thompson, who was Secretary of the Interior during Mr. Buchanan's administration and at the breaking out of the rebellion. I had known Mr. Thompson in Washington, where he was particularly [86] friendly to me in the adjustment of my long delayed accounts connected with the Mexican Boundary Commission. His predecessor, Mr. McClellan [Robert McClelland], treated me badly; as the accounts I rendered him, accompanied by explanations of certain expenditures he never examined or even opened. These accounts were found in Mr. McClellan's drawers unopened and had remained there several years, or until Mr. Thompson came into office. A resolution was then passed by Congress, leaving my accounts with the Secretary of the Interior to be adjusted by him on principles of equity and justice. After the disallowed items in my accounts had been arranged by one of the clerks under the Comptroller's direction, they were given to the Secretary, who then named an hour for me to meet him. I accordingly went there at the hour appointed, when Mr. Thompson, the Secretary examined each rejected item, heard my explanations, and read the certificates and evidences presented by me. This examination took nearly the whole day, and resulted in the allowance of all the items rejected by the examining officers 3 or 4 years before, with the exception of about $1000.[67] Mr. Thompson expressed his surprise at the time that my accounts, so well and so clearly made out, should have been subjected to such a delay, and that the suspended items had not been allowed, and the accounts adjusted years before.*

[87] I met Mr. Thompson several times after in Paris and took long walks with him. He spoke at length on the sub-

---

* Note. Mr. Secretary McClellan's bad treatment of me was owing to my discharging his brother Col. John McClellan, a miserable drunkard, from the Boundary Com. by express orders from the Secretary of the Interior.

ject of the rebellion; said he had been unjustly treated and abused, and denied the charges made against him by Mr. Seward [William Seward]. I felt great sympathy for Mr. T—— and thought him not so bad as he had been represented, but a kind hearted honorable man. I felt grateful to him for the services he had rendered me, when an entire stranger to him, and told him that if I could be of any service to him on my return, I should be most happy. I never met Mr. Thompson after my return to the United States.

Colonel Norton had frequent reunions at his house in the Champs Elysées, two of which I attended. These were very pleasant, and were attended by Europeans, as well as by the Colonels own countrymen. Was introduced to many but do not remember their names. One evening I met Major Poussin, formerly the minister accredited to the United States by the Republic under Louis Napoleon. The Major used to spend much time in New York, and was a visitor at my house. At one of my literary soirees he met my old friend Thomas Ewbank, to whom he took a great fancy, and invited Mr. Ewbank to call upon him at his hotel. Mr. E—— called on the Major the following day.

[88] I also met here Mrs. Theresa Yelverton (Lady Avonmore) an English lady of some celebrity, whom I afterwards saw in London and again on my return to Providence when she made a brief visit here.[68]

I was fortunate in being in Paris at a time when it may be said to have been in its glory. Its public buildings, parks and gardens never looked so fine, having been put in condition to receive the crowned heads of Europe, and the many thousands to view the Exposition.

After two weeks stay, I left Paris, for Geneva; thence to

Charmony [Chamonix]. Here I saw the objects most attractive to strangers, crossed the famous Mer-de-glace as most visitors do, and then returned to Geneva. While here I paid a visit to Madame Archinard and the other relatives of my son-in-law J. Antoine Duvillard, who live about three miles from the city. Leaving Geneva, I took the steamer for Lausanne; but attracted by the beauty of Ouchy and its hotel, stopped there. Thence I went to Berne, Lucerne, and Zurich. At the latter place I took the cars for Ragatz where are the celebrated Pfaffer [Pfafers] Springs and where I passed a day. Thence went by rail to Rorschach on Lake Constance, which I crossed on a steamer to Lindau on the opposite side of the lake. This is a very old town. It still has some old towers of the middle ages and a considerable [89] piece of a genuine Roman wall forty or fifty feet in height constructed of large stones. A modern stone has been inserted in the wall stating that the ancient structure was built in the fifth century. In the evening took the railway for Munich where I arrived early the following morning.

I here went to the Hotel [*blank*] where I agreed to meet Mr. Harrington [George Harrington], the United States minister, whom I saw at Berne. He was about taking a journey with Mrs. H—— and we had agreed to travel together. Found Mr. & Mrs. Harrington and took our breakfast together. We then engaged a man to act as our guide for the day, and set off for the picture gallery. It was Sunday and the gallery was closed, but a small fee induced the janitor to admit our party. Upon entering a large hall, I saw a single visitor, who had come to pass the forenoon there and, on approaching him, found it was Mr. Wm. Jones Hoppin, formerly of Providence.[69] At our hotel I found my friends Frank [*blank*] and Charles Arnold of New York. After a few days spent at Munich I went to Nuremberg in company with Mr. & Mrs. Harrington. Among the objects of interest here are the two old churches of St. Sebald [St. Sebaldus] and St. Laurence [St. Lorenz], which we visited—the old Royal Palace, Picture Gallery and Albert Durers [Albrecht Dürer's] House. Thence we went to Dresden where I passed [90] several days in the picture galleries and museums. Here I parted from Mr. & Mrs. Harrington and went to Berlin. The Egyptian museum interested me much. It contained the extensive collection of antiquities made a few years before by the Prussian expedition under Professor Lepsius [Karl Richard Lepsius] and is one of the finest in Europe. The most elegant Jewish Synagogue is in Berlin and was only recently finished. Hearing there was to be some unusual service there one afternoon, an American gentleman at our hotel joined me in taking a carriage to the synagogue. It is a magnificent edifice and is claimed to be the finest synagogue in Europe. The music was good, but I never saw in any religious edifice so little reverence. It appeared more like a business exchange than a place of worship.

Having a letter of introduction to Professor Lepsius, I took a cab and drove to his house, about a mile from the hotel. The Professor gave me a warm reception and asked many questions about America—but particularly of the aborigines and of recent archaeological researches. I asked him many questions about Egypt, by which he perceived that I was somewhat familiar with the subject. This seemed to interest him, and made him very communicative on matters relating to that country. He asked if I had visited the Egyptian Museum. [91] I replied that I had made but a par-

tial examination of the treasures it contained. He then said
if I would go there again he would join me and describe the
objects of greater interest in the collection. I had intended
to leave at noon, but the pleasure of having Prof. Lepsius as a
guide through the museum, and of hearing from his own lips
an explanation of its treasures, I determined to remain that
day. At the hour appointed the Prof. met me at the museum,
and conducted me through every portion of it, explaining its
most interesting objects. I had, of course many questions to
ask, all of which were promptly answered; such as, the earliest reliable date yet discovered, and the oldest object, the
age of which could be fixed with any degree of certainty. He
said that [the] earliest inscription or sculpture yet discovered was about 2200 or 2300 years B.C., but that he was satisfied that there were evidences in his own mind of a greater
antiquity of nearly a thousand years. He called the janitor
who brought torches, when he took me into a genuine Egyptian tomb which he had transported from Egypt, and had set
up precisely as it was in that country, with its inscriptions
and paintings. It also contained a sarcophagus, with a bust
representing the king whose body had been laid there. I do
not remember the name of the sovereign; but the Professor
said it was the most ancient portrait known.

[92] In calling afterwards at the bookstore of Asher Co.,
now kept by the Messers. Cohn, I mentioned my visit to the
museum with Prof. Lepsius. They said I must consider it a
great honor, for they never knew him to accompany any one
there before, to describe the objects, except the members of
the Royal family.

From Berlin I went to Hamburg where I remained but
one day. Thence took the railway to Brussels, which I vis-

ited the various objects of interest. I had a letter of introduction to Mr. Sanford [Henry S. Sanford] the American minister, but upon calling on him, learned that he was at Ostend
[Oostende]. Next I went to Antwerp, where I stayed four
days to attend the Anthropological Congress as a Delegate.
The attendance here was more numerous than the Congress
I attended in Paris, there being delegates present from every
country in Europe, including Turkey. Several entertain-
ments were given the members, and a grand evening fete
with fireworks, illuminations and music was got up by the
city authorities. It was one of the most brilliant affairs I ever
witnessed. Upwards of ten thousand people are said to have
been in the grounds.

The day after my arrival at Antwerp I received a letter
from Mr. Sanford, with a pressing invitation for me to return
to Brussels and pass a day with him. I according [accord-
ingly] returned to that city where I enjoyed the hospitalities
of the Minister for a day and night. Returning to Antwerp, I
took the Steamer one [93] afternoon for London, and reached
that city early in the morning of the following day. Took a
cab and drove to Mr. Henry Stevens's, Keppel Street, who
had written me while at Paris to go to his house. Mr. Stevens
was at home and received me at the door with a warm welcome from himself and Mrs. Stevens.

I remained a week or ten days in the great metropolis visiting objects and places of interest. The British Museum,
the South Kensington Museum, I visited several times, also
St. Pauls and Westminster Abbey. The latter interested me
more than any church or Cathedral in Europe, particularly
the monuments to distinguished men of whom I had heard
and read from my childhood. The Zoological Garden was also

an attractive place. Mr. and Mrs. Stevens were very kind to me, accompanying me to many places of interest. I also saw a good deal of Mr. Welford, who took me to many of the public buildings, parks, gardens etc. Mr. W. also introduced me to many of the booksellers, with some of which I had done business in former years. Among others I was shown through the large establishment of Messers. Longman & Co.

By invitation of Mr. Blackmore, I accompanied him and a party of ladies and gentlemen to Salisbury to attend the ceremonies at the dedication of the Blackmore Museum of Pre-historic times. This museum was entirely formed by Mr. Blackmore, and with its building, erected at the expense of Mr. B. was presented to the city of Salisbury. [94] On the occasion of the dedication and transfer to the city Mr. Blackmore delivered an address. Speeches were made by the Bishop of Salisbury, Lord Nelson, and other prominent men, several having come from London on the occasion. We all dined together at the "White Heart" Tavern.

The Blackmore Museum is one of the best collections in Europe illustrative of pre-historic man; in the American department I know of none that equals it. The nucleus was the fine collection of aboriginal remains from the valleys of the Mississippi and Ohio made by Messers. Squier and Davis, which being declined by several societies in New York and Boston, was purchased by Mr. Blackmore for £2,000. The collection illustrative of Swiss Lake Dwellings is also very fine. Since the founding of the museum, Mr. Blackmore has made extensive journeys in the Far West and among the Rocky Mountains and made large additions to the American department of his collection. A catalogue of the Blackmore Museum by Mr. Stevens (brother-in-law of Mr. Blackmore) illustrative of Pre-historic Archaeology, with the title of "Flint Chips" was published in London in 1870, a copy of which was presented me. The book contains a short "Preface" by me. It is very unsatisfactory to me, as it was written with the impression that it was for a small pamphlet catalogue of the Museum. Had I known the extent and importance of Mr. Stevens' work I would have written a very different article.

[95] I spent 2 or 3 days at Salisbury, visiting at the time such places of interest as were in its vicinity. Among them were Stonehenge, an interesting monument attributed to the Druids, and supposed to be of great antiquity. The great plain in the midst of which Stonehenge is situated, has still many tumuli and other earthworks which are doubtless the work of the same people who raised the huge stones for that monument. I also paid visits to Wilton House, the seat of the Earl of Pembroke; Bemerton, where Sir Philip Sidney lived, and where he wrote his "Arcadia"; where George Herbert lived and the little chapel in which he preached. Also the church erected to his memory. The beautiful cathedral at Salisbury I visited several times.

While here I made the acquaintance through Mr. & Mrs. Blackmore with several families of the place including those of Dr. H. P. Blackmore, Mr. Edward T. Stevens.

Leaving Salisbury I went to Bristol, where I passed a night and part of the following day, and thence to Bath, where I called on Mr. Moore [Charles Moore], a distinguished geologist with whom I became acquainted at Salisbury. I passed a day with Mr. Moore accompanying him to the various places of interest in Bath, which is a beautiful, though very quiet place. There is here a fine Geological Museum, formed by Mr. Moore and deposited in one of the public buildings. [96] It is particularly rich in the fossil remains of England, all collected by Mr. Moore. After dinner we made a tramp of three hours or more among the hills near the city, from which I returned excessively fatigued. Indeed, I hardly slept after it, and awoke the following morning, feeling quite ill. At 10 o'clock took the train for London, which I reached in 3 or 4 hours, and went at once to Mr. Steven's. The next day, I accompanied (by appointment) Mr. Blackmore to his house at Carshalton, a few miles from London proper, altho' within the limits of the city. I felt quite unwell, and would have preferred to remain at home, but Mr. Blackmore said he expected a number of friends to meet me; and I had promised him, when we met in Paris, to pass a few days with him.

I met at Mr. Blackmore's Mr. & Mrs. W. H. Flower, a prominent man in the learned societies of London and particularly in pre-historic subjects. Mr. [*blank*] Boyle, who had recently returned from Central America.

The next day feeling more unwell a physician was sent for, who upon seeing me said I had much fever, and must remain quiet. My illness increased and I remained at Mr. Blackmore's two weeks, part of the time in a critical state. [97] But thanks to the care and watchfulness of Mrs. Blackmore, I so far recovered as to be able to return to London. While under the roof of my kind and excellent friends at Carshalton I received calls from Bishop Clark, Dr. Shepard, and Mr. Henry T. Beckwith all of Providence, but who happened to be in London; from Mr. Welford and from Mr. & Mrs. Stevens. Returning to Mrs. Steven's, I received much care and attention from her, for I was still very weak, and unable to exert myself much. Four or five days after, I took the railway for Liverpool, where I embarked in the Inman Steamer, the City of Baltimore on the 1st October for New York, where we arrived in safety after a passage of twelve days. The same evening took the steamer for Providence, reaching home in time for breakfast the following morning.

[*The following quotation is taken from* The Patriot, *Friday Morning, March 12, 1869. It is part of a newspaper clipping Bartlett presumably saved and inserted into his autobiography. Written by the editors of the paper, the full article deals with the qualifications of the Republican candidates for state offices in Rhode Island.*]

[98] ["Rhode Island has never had a more competent or courteous Secretary of State, than John R. Bartlett, a scholar and author, who has filled his present position for fourteen years."]

[99] Papers read before the Friday evening club.[70]

Prehistoric man and his Contemporaries.
same   same (latest discoveries).
Studies of Ancient Egypt.
1869 Cuneiform Inscriptions Dec. 30, 1869
    Old Northern Runic Monuments of Scandinavia.
    Phenicia and the Phenicians.
    Psychic Force and the Phantom World.
    Etruria and the Etruscans.
    Pompeii and Herculaneum (after my visit there).
1877 Arctic Geography.
1877 The Aryan Race, its Languages, Literature and Migrations.
1878 The earliest appearance of man on the Earth;

Recent discoveries in the U. States relating thereto;
The present state of the question. Dec. 6, 1878
1879 The Libraries of the Ancients.
1880 The Exodus of the Israelites from Egypt. Dec. 3, 1880
1867 The Swiss Lake Dwellings. October 1867
1882 Bibliographers, Bibliophiles and Bibliomaniacs. Nov. 24/82
1881 The Cave and Rock Cut Temples of India. Nov. 18, 1881.
1883 Views of the most ancient people regarding immortality and the future life. Read at [*blank*].

[*Pages 100–102 are blank.*]

[103] Books illustrated by J. R. B.—that is, with
extra illustrations.[71]

1 Bryan's Dictionary of Painters & Sculptors, 2 vols. 4to, extended to ten volumes, with 2000 illustrations consisting of Portraits, and specimens of the works of the painters and sculptors. (sold to N. P. Hill, having no room for it)
2 Marshall's Life of Washington, 5 vols. 4to, extended to 10 volumes with [*blank*] illustrations.
3 Bunyan's Pilgrims Progress, extended to 3 volumes 4to.
4 Catalogue of the Library of John Carter Brown, 4 vols. royal 8vo, extended to 7. Illustrated with maps and portraits of navigators, explorers, authors, etc.
5 Cunningham's Life of Nell Gwyn, 2 vols. 4to extended, illustrated with [*blank*] portraits.
6 Ben. Perley Poore's Life and Services of General Burn-

side, extended to 2 vols. 4to illustrated with ..... Portraits, Plans of Battles, Maps, etc.

7 Parton's Life and Times of Benjamin Franklin, 2 vols., imperial 8vo extended to 4 vols., illustrated with [*blank*] portraits, etc., New York 1865. [104]

8 Drake's Dictionary of American Biography including Men of the Time, 1 vol. royal 8vo.
Illustrated with 1135 portraits, and extended to 7 volumes.

9 Memoirs of Rhode Island Officers by John R. Bartlett, one vol. 4to. Illustrated with [*blank*] portraits, Battle Scenes, Maps, etc., and extended to 2 volumes.

10 Petit's History of Mary Stuart, Queen of Scots, 2 vols. 4to, Edinburgh 1872. Illustrated with Portraits, views, etc., including portraits of Mary and of Queen Elizabeth.

11 Campbell's Life of Mary Queen of Scots, illustrated with [*blank*] portraits and extended to 2 volumes. (sold to Mrs. Ives) [*The author most likely is George Chalmers, not Campbell*]

12 Sanderson's Signers of the Declaration of Independence, 1 vol. 4to extended to 3, with [*blank*] portraits, Philadelphia 18 [*probably 1846*].

13 Sargent's Public Men and Events, 2 vols. 8vo extended to 4 vols., with [*blank*] portraits, Philadelphia 18 [1875].

14 Woodbury's Second Rhode Island Regiments, royal 8vo, L. P. with [*blank*] portraits, Providence 187– [1875].

15 Report of the Centennial Celebration of the 24th June 1865 at Pawtucket of the Incorporation of North Providence, 4to large paper, Prov. 1865. Illustrated with portraits & plates.

[105] 16. Genl. McClellan's Report on the army of the Potomac Aug. 4, 1863, with an account of the campaign in

Western Virginia, Royal 8vo, extended to 2 vols., Large paper, & illustrated with 94 portraits and other plates. An edition of 100 copies in this form royal 8vo was printed at the expense of General McClellan's friends in New York and presented to him. This is a copy of the edition. The plates were all added by me.

17 Charles Deane's Memoir of George Livermore, prepared by order of the Massachusetts Historical Society, 4to, Large Paper, Cambridge 1869. Illustrated with 42 portraits & other plates.

18 Campbell's Gertrude of Wyoming: A Pennsylvanian Tale & other poems, 4to, London 1809. Illustrated with 55 plates and an autograph letter of the author.

19 Life and Services of Edward Everett. An address delivered before the citizens of Cambridge, February 22, 1865. By Richard H. Dana Jr., 4to Large paper (55 copies printed) Cambridge 1865. Illustrated with 40 illustrations.

[106] 20 An Oration on the annals of Rhode Island and Providence Plantations by the Rev. Francis Vinton D.D.; and a Rhyme of Rhode Island and the Times, By George William Curtis. Delivered before the Sons of Rhode Island in New York, May 29, 1863, 4to, New York 1864. Illustrated with portraits and other plates. 68 illustrations.

21 The Book-Hunter. By John Hill Burton, 4to Large paper, Edinburgh and London 1872. Illustrated with 200 portraits and other plates. Extended to 2 volumes 4to.

[*Pages 107–108 are blank.*]

[*The following section appears to have been written in about 1885. Several of the items are chronologically out of order with respect to the rest of the autobiography.*]

[109] <u>Additional notes</u>. At Ellen's request that I should make a few notes or memoranda of incidents in my life of which no mention is made in the foregoing notes I add them here. She has suggested them to me.

<u>Edgar A. Poe</u>. While residing in N.Yk. between 1837 and 1849 I became acquainted with Mr. Poe. I saw him during the years he spent there very often, and sometimes daily while my place of business was in the Astor House. He also visited my house. Mrs. Frances S. Osgood was a frequent [visitor] there, and when she was with my family Poe called every day, and generally spent the evening, remaining invariably until midnight.[72] One evening he attended a soirée of literary men such as I frequently had. On these occasions I gave my simple repasts of bread & butter, cake, tea & coffee. The evening after Mr. Poe called and said he drank the previous evening such delicious coffee and so much of it that he sat up the whole night in writing, and that he had then called to ask for another cup of the same. I ordered the coffee made expressly for him, of which he partook liberally.

[*1872, Second European Trip*]

[110] Ellen desires me to note down some incidents of my second visit to Europe in which she and Fanny accompanied me. The incidents worth mentioning are few and scarcely worth recording. We sailed from New York on the [6] June 1873 [1872] in the steamer [City of Baltimore] and had a pleasant passage to Liverpool. Hastening on to London, we put up at Mrs. [Nugent's] No. [24] Montague Street opposite the British Museum, where we were well accommodated.[73]

We remained several weeks in London during which time we visited the numerous places of interest for which the city is famous. We also visited Beford [Bedford] and Salisbury. From the latter place we drove out to Stonehenge, being my second visit to that interesting place. It is here that those remarkable remains attributed to the ancient Druids are found. Also visited Old Sarum equally famous with Stonehenge. Nothing, however, remains here but vast earthworks, over and around which we rambled. Took tea while at Salisbury with Dr. Blackmore, a brother of Mr. William Blackmore, my old friend, whom I visited when before in England.

One day we attended a garden party at Mr. Henry G. Bohn just out of London. A large number were present including many dignitaries. Among them were an Indian [111] king and his son. His name, a very long one, I do not remember. They wore their oriental costumes. I noticed an elderly gentleman whom I at once recognized from the portraits I had seen of him as Sir John Bowring, formerly the British minister in Siam, and the author of several books on the East. But he is better known in the United States for his translations of foreign poetry, particularly the Russian in which appears that remarkable one by Derzavin [Gavril R. Derzhavin], entitled "Ode to God." The gentleman to whom I said that I recognized Sir John from his engraved portrait, crossed the garden and told him what I had said. He at once brought this gentleman and introduced him to us. We had a pleasant talk, in which many questions were asked us about America. I told Sir John that his beautiful poem from the Russian of Derzavin [Derzhavin] was well known among us, and that I know several gentlemen who could repeat the whole. That

FIGURE 12

John Russell Bartlett, an oil painting by John Knowlton Arnold, 1871. This painting was done near the end of Bartlett's long tenure as Secretary of State and at a time when Bartlett was actively preparing the catalogues of the Bibliotheca Americana for John Carter Brown. His hair on the original painting is light reddish-brown with some gray on the temples, suggesting he might have been applying a tint to cover the more pronounced gray that appears on earlier portraits of him. Looking supremely self-assured, Bartlett has chosen to have his portrait taken while sitting in a high-back red chair, with five books aligned on a small table next to him. From left to right the volumes are: (1) a published hardback with *Egypt* printed on the spine, a book by Karl Richard Lepsius, the noted German Egyptologist who in 1867 gave Bartlett a personally guided tour of his museum in Berlin; (2) another published hardback with *Antiquity of Man* printed on the spine, one of many editions of a book written by Sir Charles Lyell and published by John Murray of London. Considered by many to be the father of modern geology, Lyell probably met Bartlett at the antiquities conferences both men attended in Europe in 1867; (3) a self-bound book or scrapbook, perhaps the original manuscript of *Memoirs of Rhode Island Officers*, whose title has been hand-printed on the spine by Bartlett; (4) a self-bound soft cover with an illegible title printed in Bartlett's hand; (5) another self-bound soft cover with what appears to have *Historical Magazine* and *Quotes and Queries* as a hand-printed title on its cover. Courtesy of the John Carter Brown Library.

FIGURE 12

FIGURE 13

Major Henry Anthony Bartlett, U.S. Marine Corps. This photograph follows p. 134 of the *Russell Family Genealogy*, a volume published by J. R. Bartlett in 1879. Given a probable date of ca. 1878 for the photo, Henry Bartlett would have been approximately 40 years old at the time this picture was taken.

FIGURE 14

Commander John Russell Bartlett, Jr., U.S. Navy. This photograph follows p. 136 of the *Russell Family Genealogy*, a book published by J. R. Bartlett in 1879. John Bartlett, Jr., would have been approximately 35 years old at the time the photo was taken. He was later promoted to Captain while on active duty and to Rear Admiral while on the list of retired officers.

FIGURE 15

This undated photograph of John Russell Bartlett, taken by R. A. Lewis
of New York City, is the original from which the engraving of Bartlett
was made for the *Russell Family Genealogy* published in 1879. Bartlett's
advancing age is more apparent in this photo than on the Arnold painting
of 1871 (Figure 12), but not as advanced as those shown on an 1879 photo
of Bartlett (Figure 16). Thus, a tentative date of ca. 1875 is assigned to
this photo. Courtesy of the John Carter Brown Library.

FIGURE 16

A contemplative John Russell Bartlett poses for the camera of the Manches-
ter Brothers of Providence in this photograph dated from 1879. Although
Bartlett's hair and beard are distinctly whiter than they appear on earlier
photos and drawings, his hairline has remained virtually unchanged since
1850. Courtesy of the John Carter Brown Library.

FIGURE 17

An oil portrait of John Russell Bartlett by James Sullivan Lincoln. Based upon a ledger of portraits found among the artist's papers (MSS 537) at the Rhode Island Historical Society Library, we can surmise that Lincoln made this painting in either March 1883 or June 1884. Bartlett paid Lincoln $75.00 for the portrait—half of Lincoln's normal rate for paintings of this size. Although by this time Bartlett's hair and beard are thoroughly whitened by age, the intellectual fire still burns brightly in his eyes. There is an excellent copy of this painting that was donated by Major Henry Anthony Bartlett, Bartlett's son, to the Rhode Island Historical Society in 1894. Purportedly, Henry Bartlett's second wife, Cara Hall Bartlett, made the copy. The original painting by Lincoln is reproduced here through the generosity of its owner, the Providence Athenaeum.

FIGURE 17

JOHN R. BARTLETT

FIGURE 18

I had read it many times and thought I could then repeat the larger part of it. I told him that about once in every ten years it found its way into some newspaper, and generally went the rounds of hundreds of papers, all wondering who wrote it. It was not long however before his name as the translator was made known.[74] I met Sir John a few days later at the Prison Congress to which I was a delegate. The Convention or Congress [112] was held in the Inner Temple. He was on the raised platform and discovering me and my wife and daughter came and took a seat near us. He died soon after we left London.

Another acquaintance we made at Mr. Bohns was Sir Sidney Waterlow, who, soon after became Lord Mayor of London. We had much to say to him and found him a most intelligent and agreeable gentleman. He introduced us to Lady Waterlow. By appointment he called for us with his carriage the following day and took us [to] Holloway Prison, of which he was one of the founders. He introduced us to the Governor of the prison, who showed us every part of it. We were struck with the good order and cleanliness of it. Sir Sidney afterwards took us in his carriage to some of the model tenement houses which he had built and which were considered the finest and most convenient of their kind in London.

In speaking of Sir John Bowring's poem from the Russian entitled "Ode to God," I ought to have given its beginning as by that it will be more readily recognized. It begins:

FIGURE 18 (*opposite*). Nattily attired and sporting a goatee, a very serious looking John Russell Bartlett poses for the camera in this undated photograph from ca. 1885. Courtesy the Rhode Island Historical Society. Rhi x3 540.

"Oh thou Eternal One, whose presence bright
All space doth occupy, all motion guide
Who fills't existence with thyself alone"

[113] Dr. E. M. Snow, of Providence, who was associated with me as one of the delegates to the Prison Congress passed an evening with us, also the Rev. Dr. Caldwell of Providence.

Took dinner at Mr. Rathbone's [William Rathbone], member of Parliament. I do not remember the names of those we met there.

Among the pleasant acquaintances made in London was that of George Cruikshank the famous artist and caricaturist. Having a letter of introduction I called upon him and [was] most kindly received. Was introduced to Mrs. Cruikshank. Passed a pleasant hour with him listening to his early reminiscences. They asked my wife and self to tea a day or two later, but she was unable to go. I went, took tea and remained during the evening. Again he referred to his early life, of his drinking habit, of his thorough reform and of his becoming a te-totaller. He said that his business as an artist was ruined by the course he had taken against the use of spiritual liquors. On the death of Mr. Cruikshank soon after my return, I wrote a particular account of my visit to him, in which I related all he told me of his early life. My article I sent to the Providence Journal. Mr. Danielson [George W. Danielson, editor] did not think proper to print it. Several friends in New York, admirers of Cruikshank, [114] having heard that I had made his acquaintance wrote me, urging me to write out my recollections of him and have them printed.

I accordingly took [the manuscript] from the Journal Office where it had lain six weeks, and sent it to my friends in New York who took it to Mr. Bryant [William Cullen Bryant, editor], at the office of the [New York] Evening Post. It was published the following day. I think I saved a copy of the article which is among my papers.

Very soon after the great battle of Gettysburg steps were taken by the State of Pennsylvania to preserve the battle-ground and make arrangements for a National Cemetery. These proceedings were followed by the formation of an association of all the loyal States for a National Cemetery, into which was merged the State association. The Governor of Rhode Island appointed me the member to represent the State. The first meeting of the association took place at Gettysburg four months after the battle, when an organization took place. I was elected Secretary of the Board of Managers and attended its meetings. I think they took place once in every three months. At the formal dedication or consecration of the cemetery, President Lincoln, the members of his Cabinet, and a number of distinguished men were present. The oration was delivered by Edward Everett. It was on this occasion that [115] President Lincoln made the opening address or remarks which have immortalized him. We sat on the raised platform at the end of a seat within ten feet of Mr. Lincoln & Mr. Everett. The President said:

"Four score and seven years ago our fathers brought forth upon this continent a new nation, conceived in Liberty, and dedicated to the proposition that all men are created equal. Now we are engaged in a great civil

war, testing whether that nation or any nation so conceived and so dedicated can long endure. We are met on
a great battle-field of that war. We are met to dedicate
a portion of it as the final resting place of those who
gave their lives that that nation might live. It is alto-
gether fitting & proper that we should do this.

But in a larger sense we cannot dedicate, we cannot
consecrate, we cannot hallow this ground. The brave
men living and dead, who struggled here have conse-
crated it far above our power to add or detract. The
world will little note, nor long remember what we say
here, but it will never forget what they did here. It is
for us, the living, rather to be dedicated here to the
unfinished work that they have thus far so nobly carried on. It is rather for us to be here dedicated to the
great task remaining before us, that from these honored dead we take increased devotion to the cause for
which they here gave the last full measure of devotion,
that we here highly resolve that the dead shall not have
died in vain; that the nation shall, under God, have a
new birth of freedom, and that the government of the
people, by the people, and for the people, shall not per-
ish from the earth."[75]

[116] When the Prince of Wales visited this country in 18
[1860] he landed at Quebec. As it was a part of his plans to
visit New York and Boston, an effort was made to induce
him to visit Providence. Gov. Sprague was particularly anx-
ious that he should come, and directed me to proceed to
Quebec, with proper credentials, and be there at the time of
his arrival. Mr. Byron Sprague accompanied me. We waited

five days at Quebec for the arrival of the ship that bore his Royal Highness. I was on the platform when he landed and thus had a good view of him.[76]

The following day we took a carriage and drove out to the Governor's residence where the Prince was staying to carry Governor Sprague's invitation. The Duke of Newcastle received us, and we were presented to several of the gentlemen of the prince's suite; but we did not see His Royal Highness. We remained half an hour in conversation with the various gentlemen, who were extremely inquisitive about various places they wished to see. The White Mountains, in particular interested them.

I could not then get an answer [to] the invitation I bore, as they said the party was entirely in the hands of Lord Lyons [Richard Bickerton Pemell Lyons], the British Minister at Washington, who had doubtless made all the plans and laid out the routes to be travelled. [117] A few days after my return home, I received a letter from the Duke of Newcastle, regretting that the Prince could not visit Providence, as the plans & miles had already been agreed upon, which did not include Providence, and the day of sailing from Portland had also been fixed.

APPENDICES

A Legacy of Art

Some writers have suggested that Bartlett probably gave up painting after his Boundary Commission days of the 1850s, in large part because his attention was consumed by his official duties as Secretary of State, the preparation of his catalogues for John Carter Brown, and his other writing and publishing projects. However, this is not the case. The Rhode Island Historical Society Library has twenty-six watercolors by Bartlett, three of which are clearly signed, "J. R. Bartlett," and dated, "1880," on the recto of the drawings. Thus, we have dated and signed artwork by Bartlett that extends from his 1828 sepia and wash of Barre, the rescue dog at the Convent of St. Bernard, to several of the Bartlett watercolors at the RIHS that date from 1880. Moreover, it is a virtual certainty that he produced other artwork that precedes 1828.

The watercolors at the Rhode Island Historical Society have the following numerical sequence and titles. According to Dana S. Munroe of the RIHS Library, most of the untitled watercolors are scenes from Martha's Vineyard.

1. The title of this work appears on the verso, *The Geysers—California*, followed by the notation, "By J. R. Bartlett." This scene is a view upstream (southeast) along Big Sulphur Creek in the Mayacmas Mountains of northern California. Depicted is a swift-flowing river on the canyon floor, four men with a freshly killed deer on a rocky promontory in the foreground, and three men in the background who are inspecting a series of active fumaroles or steam vents that

issue from a steep slope north of the river. The Bartlett Collection at the John Carter Brown Library has both the original pencil field sketch (no. 172 L) of this scene, taken by Bartlett on March 23, 1852, and Bartlett's sepia and wash version (no. 57). The latter forms the basis of the lithograph that follows p. 40, vol. 2, of *Personal Narrative*. In 2002, a large-format copy of the watercolor version of *The Geysers* became the showpiece of the first permanent public display of Bartlett artwork: *John Russell Bartlett: An Artist's View of The Geysers, March 1852*, curated by Jerry E. Mueller, Mark A. Walters, and Michele Botarro-Walters, an interpretive exhibit of eight drawings at the Geothermal Visitors Center, Middletown, California.

2. The title of this drawing is, *Scene in the Arctic Regions*, followed by the notation, "Position of the ship." Bartlett used a series of very dark grays and whites to fashion his scene. This watercolor is unusual in two respects. First, it is the only drawing in the collection, other than the California scene in number 1, that is from outside the southern New England area. Second, it is the only scene in the sequence that is taken from a locality that Bartlett assuredly never visited. In fact, *Scene in the Arctic Regions* seems to have been based on, or inspired by, *Entering Lancaster Sound*, an engraved drawing used as a frontispiece to Elisha Kent Kane's, *The U. S. Grinnell Expedition in Search of Sir John Franklin* (New York: Harper & Brothers, 1854). There is a distinct possibility Bartlett prepared his watercolor as a visual aid to accompany his lectures on the Arctic region: he presented one such lecture to the Friday Evening Club on December 8, 1876; a second lecture was given before the Rhode Island Historical Society on February 13, 1877. *Scene in the Arctic*

Regions might also be related to some of Bartlett's biblio-graphic work on the polar regions.

3. This drawing is labeled, *Squantum*, by "J. R. Bartlett." The drawing is exceptionally well done. It employs pencil and pencil shading in the background and middle ground, and in the foreground, ink has also been used. Squantum refers to a private club that was established in 1872 on an island on the east side of the Providence River, but which is now connected by a causeway to the mainland. Although Bartlett, as Secretary of State, signed the original incorpo-ration papers for the Squantum Association, he apparently was never a member of the club. However, many of his close associates were, including Henry B. Anthony, Bartlett's brother-in-law; William Sprague, politician and industrial-ist; James Bucklin, architect; and John Nicholas Brown, son of John Carter Brown. See Robert E. Anderson, *The History of Squantum on the Occasion of the 100th Anniversary of the Incorpo-ration of the Association* (Providence: Squantum Association, May 3, 1972).

4. This very clean and well-done scene is labeled, *Squan-tum from the Bridge*. On the verso is written, "Squantum from the Bridge leading to Huckleberry Island." In this view to the northwest, Bartlett captures a portion of Squantum Point, a small, undeveloped, conical island of 2.74 acres, beyond which is a much larger island that houses the main facilities of the Squantum Association. Squantum is located a few miles south/southeast of Providence and is accessible from Veterans Memorial Parkway in East Providence (see Fig. 27).

5. This scene is titled, *Squantum from the south*, on the verso of the drawing.

6. The pencil title to this drawing is, *A Study*.

7. This drawing carries the title, *View Near Narragansett Pier*. Narragansett is located along the west shore of Narragansett Bay, approximately 25 miles south of Providence.

8. *Rocks at Narragansett Pier* is the title of this drawing.

9. The title on the front of this drawing is *Gay Head*. This drawing is signed and dated in ink, "J. R. Bartlett 1880." "Gay Head" also appears in pencil on the verso of the drawing. The scene in this drawing is taken from the western extremity of Martha's Vineyard, a large island off the south coast of Massachusetts.

10. This untitled drawing is probably from Martha's Vineyard.

11. This untitled drawing is also likely taken from Martha's Vineyard. It is signed and dated in ink on the lower right of the recto of the drawing, "J. R. Bartlett 1880."

12. This untitled drawing is also likely taken from Martha's Vineyard.

13. Another untitled drawing that was likely taken from Martha's Vineyard.

14. Another untitled drawing that was likely taken from Martha's Vineyard.

15. This watercolor carries the title, *The Forty Steps—Newport Cliffs*. Newport is located at the south end of Aquidneck Island, also known as Rhode Island, a large island at the south end of Narragansett Bay, approximately 25 miles south-southeast of Providence. The Forty Steps are located almost directly south of Newport at 41° 28' 33" N. Lat., 71° 17' 50" W. Long.

16. *View from Paradise Rocks—Newport* is the title of this scene. Paradise Rocks form a series of streamlined glacial

hills located east of Newport at 41° 30' 04" N. Lat., 71° 15' 46" W. Long.

17. The title of this drawing is, *Portrait of a tree near Mr. Jencke's* [,] *Lonsdale*. The reference here is likely to Thomas Allen Jenckes (1818–1875), a native Rhode Islander and a graduate of Brown University. Jenckes was a prominent lawyer in Providence and New York, a Rhode Island legislator, and a Congressman from the state.

18. This watercolor is titled, *Old Stone Mill. Newport*. The Old Stone Mill is a circular, man-made structure located in Touro Park in Newport. Its origin has been debated for hundreds of years, with the most prevalent theory that it dates from early colonial days. However, there are other authorities who suggest this landmark has a Norse origin. The controversy surrounding the origin of the mill in part accounts for its being a favorite subject for artists and photographers (see Fig. 28).

19. The title of this drawing is, *Near the Ocean Drive—Newport*. In this scene, a small boat is left unfinished by the artist.

20. *Ocean Drive—Newport* is the title on the front of this drawing.

21. This watercolor carries the title, *View overlooking Lily Pond—Newport*. Lily Pond is located southwest of Newport on the Newport Neck, at 41° 27' 47" N. Lat., 71° 19' 16" W. Long.

22. The pencil title of this scene is, *Hanging Rock, Newport, from the South*. Hanging Rock is another streamlined glacial hill located east of Newport at 41° 29' 29" N. Lat., 71° 15' 32" W. Long.

23. This drawing is titled, *Hanging Rock, Newport*.

24. *Seekonk River* is the pencil title of this watercolor. The Seekonk River is an estuary that separates East Providence from Providence. It joins the Providence River at the head of the Providence Harbor.

25. This scene is untitled and its location is unknown.

26. Another untitled scene with an unknown location. It, too, displays a boat that was left unfinished by Bartlett.

John Carter Brown and the Bibliotheca Americana

John Carter Brown (1797–1874) was descended from a very prominent Providence family that amassed a fortune in trade, textiles, and other ventures. His grandfather, Nicholas Brown (1729–1791), was a founder and benefactor of the Providence Library Company, serving as that organization's first librarian from 1753 to 1762. John Carter Brown's father, Nicholas Brown, Jr., (1769–1841), served as Board President of the Providence Library Company from 1807 to 1812, and his generosity to his alma mater, Rhode Island College, was recognized in 1804 when the school changed its name to Brown University. John Carter Brown, himself a graduate of Brown University, was a member or subscriber of the Providence Library Company at least as early as 1826, by which time he had started his own collection of fine books. Thus, the pattern of education, books, public service, and philanthropy that characterizes the Browns was already well established prior to 1830.

FIGURE 19

John Carter Brown added this wing to the Nightingale-Brown House in 1862 in order to hold his ever-expanding Bibliotheca Americana, a book collection that Brown built with the aid of his librarian, John Russell Bartlett. It was from this room that Bartlett produced his magnificent catalogues of the Bibliotheca Americana between 1865 and 1882. In his book, *Private Libraries of Providence* (1878), Horatio Rogers states:

> The library room in the Brown mansion, having been built expressly for the purpose, is practically fire-proof. Most of the light comes from above, for a single door and two windows alone break the walls, which are lined with heavily-laden book shelves. Turkish rugs are spread upon the tessellated floor, and four or five marble busts and figures upon pedestals lend elegance to the literary appearance of the room. All of the books are exposed to an unobstructed view, save those in a single case which are covered with

(*continues*)

It is not known when John Russell Bartlett first met John Carter Brown. However, there is enough circumstantial evidence to suggest a date from the late 1820s when both young men were involved with the Providence Library Company—Brown as a subscriber and user of the facility, and Bartlett as a user and donor, for the latter gave the library $5.00 on May 11, 1829, towards a subscription to the *New York Gazette* ("Treasurer's Account from September 1828 to September 1829," unpublished records of the Providence Library Company held by the Providence Athenaeum). At the same time, both men were involved in local banking, John Russell Bartlett as a clerk for Cyrus Butler at the Bank of North America, and John Carter Brown and his father, Nicholas Brown, Jr., as directors of the Providence Bank. In 1831, almost immediately after Bartlett, Frederick Farley, and Thomas Webb founded the Providence Athenaeum, discussions began about a possible merger of the Athenaeum with the Providence Library Company, a venerable institution long supported by the Browns. When the merger was effected in 1836, John Russell Bartlett and John Carter Brown became charter members of the "new" Athenaeum. Thus, there are several lines of evidence to suggest that Bartlett

---

FIGURE 19 (*cont.*)

glass. [Quoted in John D. Haskell, Jr., "John Russell Bartlett (1805–1886): Bookman." Ph.D. dissertation, George Washington University, 1977, p. 204).

The much-restored Nightingale-Brown House, a National Historic Landmark, is now owned by Brown University. Presently it houses the John Nicholas Brown Center for the Study of American Civilization. The library addition of 1862 is utilized as an all-purpose room by the Center. Photo by Jerry E. Mueller.

FIGURE 20

This photograph was taken at Niagara Falls in 1874, after the death of John
Carter Brown. Standing left to right are Brown's two young sons, John
Nicholas Brown (age 12) and Harold Brown (age 10). Seated left to right
are John Russell Bartlett and the French tutor of the young Browns, Mr.
M. Surlean. Bartlett apparently served as surrogate father to the Brown
sons after the death of their father, educating and guiding them in the
business of collecting fine books, thus allowing the boys to follow in their
father's footsteps and further build the Bibliotheca Americana, the great
collection that would ultimately become the John Carter Brown Library.
Courtesy of the John Carter Brown Library.

and Brown were well acquainted long before Bartlett began to help John Carter Brown build his Bibliotheca Americana into a world-class personal library.

The earliest correspondence between Bartlett and Brown demonstrates that John Carter Brown was doing business in 1845 with the bookstore of Bartlett & Welford in New York City. There is other correspondence on book matters between the two men leading up to Bartlett's appointment to the Mexican Boundary Survey in 1850. After a hiatus of three years, the correspondence resumes in December 1853, shortly after Bartlett returned to Providence from his father's house in Cape Vincent, New York, to which he had retreated months earlier to prepare the manuscript for his *Personal Narrative*. The correspondence between Bartlett and Brown continues to the time of Brown's death in 1874; thereafter, there is much correspondence on book matters between Bartlett and Brown's survivors—wife Sophia Augusta Brown (1825–1909), and sons, John Nicholas Brown (1861–1900) and Harold Brown (1865–1900)—until Bartlett's death in 1886. Thus Bartlett is rightly considered to be the first librarian of the John Carter Brown Library, beginning in approximately 1855 and continuing in this capacity until his own death in 1886.

Bartlett's contribution to the growth and development of John Carter Brown's Bibliotheca Americana was enormous and manifested itself in the great number of roles Bartlett assumed for the Browns. That he was able to do so, especially during the first seventeen years when he was also Secretary of State, is a testament to Bartlett's experience, accomplishments, and stature as a bookman in the years leading up to his direct involvement in John Carter Brown's library.

Brown provided wealth and a good business and investment sense to the building of his book collection; Bartlett added his knowledge of printing, publishing, book dealers, book collectors, and auction houses to their union. Together, they forged a formidable team of the knowledgable and discriminating collector and the consummate bookman. For John Carter Brown, the Bibliotheca Americana was to be his legacy, and his name would forever be associated with one of the world's great research libraries. For John Russell Bartlett, the Bibliotheca Americana would provide an outlet for his immense intellectual appetite, especially during the long period in which he was largely occupied with the more mundane duties of attending to state matters. How fortunate for John Carter Brown and the Brown family, as well as the Bibliotheca Americana and the eventual establishment of the John Carter Brown Library, that Bartlett was a state official who served for such a long and uninterrupted period of time, followed by an almost equally long period of retirement in which Bartlett's participation in the library remained steadfast.

A brief chronology of events in the early history of the John Carter Brown Library, 1814–1904, follows:

1814 Nicholas Brown, Jr., the father of John Carter Brown, buys the Nightingale House at what is now 357 Benefit Street in Providence. It is here that the younger Brown would live the rest of his life, building his great collection of books on colonial America—the Bibliotheca Americana.

1845 In the earliest known correspondence between the two men, John Carter Brown writes to John Russell

Bartlett of Bartlett and Welford Bookstore, New York City, to thank Bartlett for his assistance in obtaining some Bibles.

1849 John Carter Brown writes and invites Bartlett to visit the Bibliotheca Americana in Providence.

1855 The probable year Bartlett becomes private librarian to John Carter Brown.

1862 John Carter Brown adds a wing to the northeast corner of his house to hold his expanding personal library (see Fig. 19).

1865 Bartlett produces the first printed catalogue of Brown's library: *Bibliotheca Americana: A Catalogue of Books Relating to North and South America in the Library of John Carter Brown. Part I. 1493 to 1600.* With Notes by John Russell Bartlett (Providence, 1865).

1866 Bartlett finishes Part II (1601–1700) of the catalogue of the Bibliotheca Americana.

1870 Bartlett completes volume I (1701–1771) of Part III of the catalogue of Brown's Library.

1871 Bartlett produces volume II (1772–1800) of Part III of the Bibliotheca Americana.

1873 A codicil dated June 12, 1873, is added to the will of John Carter Brown dated December 30, 1867. Item 2 of the codicil provides cash bequests to several local organizations plus one individual outside the Brown family: "I give and bequeath unto my friend John R. Bartlett, the sum of Five thousand ($5,000.00); to be paid within one year from the time of my decease."

1874 John Carter Brown dies, and the control of the library passes to Brown's widow, Sophia Augusta Brown, who retains Bartlett as librarian. It has been said that

Bartlett became a surrogate father to John Carter Brown's two sons, John Nicholas Brown and Harold Brown, and nurtured them in the art of collecting fine books [Fig. 20].

1874? In her will, Sophia Augusta Brown directs that, should John Nicholas Brown and Harold Brown die before they can legally assume title to the Bibliotheca Americana, the book collection should go to Brown University, where it would be kept intact and be forever known as the "John Carter Brown Library."

1875 Bartlett publishes a revised and greatly expanded catalogue for Part I (1492–1600) of John Carter Brown's library.

1876 The Centennial Exposition in Philadelphia awards Bartlett a medal for his bibliographic work on the catalogues of the Bibliotheca Americana.

1880 John Russell Bartlett donates his Mexican Boundary Commission papers to Sophia Augusta Brown and the Bibliotheca Americana.

1882 Bartlett publishes his revised and greatly expanded catalogue for Part II (1601–1700) of the Brown family library.

1886 John Russell Bartlett dies. Sophia Augusta, John Nicholas, and Harold Brown continue to acquire rare books for the family library.

1895 George Parker Winship is hired by the Browns as the first full-time librarian of the Bibliotheca Americana.

1898 Sophia Brown awards legal title to the Bibliotheca Americana to her oldest son, John Nicholas Brown.

1900 Disaster strikes as John Nicholas Brown and Harold Brown die just ten days apart, both in their thirties.

1901 Following the dictates of the will of John Nicholas Brown, the two trustees of the Bibliotheca Americana, George W. R. Matteson and Robert H. I. Goddard, arrange for the legal transfer of the library to Brown University, with the stipulation that the library would not only remain intact, but would also be independently housed and administered.

1902 Although John Nicholas Brown had earlier devised elaborate plans for a stand-alone library behind the Nightingale-Brown house at 357 Benefit Street, the trustees of the library and the Brown family agree to house the Bibliotheca Americana in its own building on the main quadrangle at Brown University.

1904 The John Carter Brown Library dedicates its new quarters, a limestone classical building at the southeast corner of the main quadrangle at Brown University.

The information on the history of the John Carter Brown Library is taken from a variety of sources that include:

The History of the State of Rhode Island and Providence Plantations: Biographical (New York: The American Historical Society, Inc., vol. 6, 1920).

MSS127–Thomas A. Jenckes Papers, Rhode Island Historical Society Library. Box 6 contains copies of the wills of John Carter Brown and Sophia Augusta Brown.

Richard J. Ring, "The Bibliotheca Americana Comes to Brown University: One Hundredth Anniversary, 1901–2001," an unpublished catalogue of an exhibition held at the John Carter Brown Library, November–December 2001.

George Parker Winship, *The John Carter Brown Library: A History* (Providence 1914).

Awards and Recognition

John Russell Bartlett was known as a humble and unostentatious person. Yet from his writing we know it was important to him that he be recognized in Reuben Guild's *History of Brown University* (1867) for his efforts at securing the large collection of portraits of Rhode Island's early leaders. We also know Bartlett took great pride in having received all of the votes for Secretary of State in the Rhode Island elections of 1860. At the same time, he apparently disregarded other honors, recognition, and awards, at least to the point of not mentioning them in his autobiography. For example, one of his greatest honors was the honorary Master of Arts bestowed upon him in 1848 by President Francis Wayland of Brown University, in recognition of Bartlett's scholarly contributions, in particular, his *Progress of Ethnology* (1847) and the *Dictionary of Americanisms* (1848). A good question is, "How could anyone neglect to mention in an autobiography his/her honorary degree from Brown University?" Although Bartlett enjoys at least a regional reputation in New England and the Southwest, few would know today that he served as Acting Governor of Rhode Island in 1861–1862 when Governor William Sprague IV was on leave to fight in the Civil War. One could argue that Bartlett served as acting governor according to the law and not by choice, but such service is an honor nonetheless, and his failure to mention this phase of his career in his autobiography is somewhat puzzling.

We also know from an examination of Bartlett's list of publications that at least four important works by him were not included, with one or two of the omissions probably intentional. But at least two of the books were entirely non-controversial and worthy of inclusion; these are, *Census of the Inhabitants of the Colony of Rhode Island and Providence Plantations* (1858) and *The Soldiers' National Cemetery at Gettysburg* (1874). The Gettysburg volume is a compilation of materials Bartlett collected during the many years he served as secretary of the Board of Commissioners for the Soldiers' National Cemetery, an interstate association that eventually oversaw the transfer of the cemetery from the State of Pennsylvania to the Federal government. Given that John Russell Bartlett, his second wife, Ellen Eddy Bartlett, and his youngest daughter, Fanny Osgood Bartlett, had the honor of sharing the platform from which Abraham Lincoln delivered his Gettysburg Address on November 19, 1863, it is all the more enigmatic that Bartlett should have neglected to include the Gettysburg volume in his list of publications.

Lastly, Bartlett received an honor of national significance fairly late in his career, a medal at the 1876 Centennial Exposition held in Philadelphia. This medal, held by the John Carter Brown Library, was awarded to Bartlett for his preparation of the catalogues of the Bibliotheca Americana. It seems a fitting tribute to Bartlett that this last honor, also not mentioned by him in his autobiography, recognized him for his talent and productivity as a bibliophile. It is also fitting and appropriate that the bibliophiles of Providence would unite in 1983, nearly a hundred years after the death of Bartlett, to form the John Russell Bartlett Society. That society participated in the induction of John Russell Bartlett into the Rhode Island Heritage Hall of Fame on October 23, 2004.

Closure

The Bartlett family plot is located on the far east side of Swan Point Cemetery, a large, park-like facility that is located east of Blackstone Boulevard in Providence. John Russell Bartlett (1805–1886) and his first wife, Eliza A. Bartlett (1810–1853), and their three children who died in childhood, Leila (1846–1850), George Francis (1840–1842), and Elizabeth Dorrance (1833–1840), are buried in a row, their graves marked with simple and highly deteriorated marble slabs placed flat on the ground. Near the center of the plot is a large block of granite on which "John R. Bartlett" is inscribed. When facing west and to the left of Bartlett's grave, there is a monument that marks the graves of Bartlett's grandson, Henry A. Duvillard (1859–1943) and his wife, Margaret D. Duvillard (1863–1948), and beyond them is the grave of Bartlett's daughter, Anna Russell Bartlett Duvillard (1835–1885). In the far left of the plot are the graves of John Russell Bartlett, Jr., (1843–1904) and his wife, Jeanie R. Jenckes Bartlett (1844–1907). The only graves in the far right of the plot are those of Elisha Capron Mowry (1882–1978), a distinguished Providence lawyer, and his wife, Ida Russell Bartlett Mowry (1875–1964), the daughter of John Russell Bartlett, Jr. Of the two Bartlett children who are not buried in Swan Point,

Fanny Osgood Bartlett (1850–1882) is buried in New York, and Henry A. Bartlett (1838–1901) is buried in Arlington National Cemetery. The only known living descendents of John Russell Bartlett are derived from Ida Bartlett Mowry and Eleanor Bartlett Edwards (1882–1920), the two daughters of John Russell Bartlett, Jr. For most of their adult lives, Ida Mowry resided in Providence, Rhode Island, and Eleanor Edwards lived on a ranch in southern Colorado.

Additional Sources on the Life of John Russell Bartlett

William Gammell, "Life and services of the Hon. John Russell Bartlett: A Paper read before the Rhode Island Historical Society on November 2, 1886" (Providence: Providence Press Company, 1886).

John D. Haskell, Jr., "John Russell Bartlett: Bookman." Ph.D. dissertation, George Washington University, 1977.

Elisha Capron Mowry, "John Russell Bartlett," a paper read before the Review Club, January 12, 1957, Providence. This is an unpublished manuscript written by Bartlett's grandson-in-law, who was married to Ida Russell Bartlett, the daughter of John Russell Bartlett, Jr.

NOTES

NOTES

1. Smith Bartlett was born April 24, 1780, and died in Cape Vincent, New York, on November 11, 1867, shortly after the bulk of this autobiography was written. Nancy Russell Bartlett was born July 17, 1782, in Providence, Rhode Island, and married Smith Bartlett on September 26, 1802. She died February 11, 1819, in Kingston, Ontario, when John Russell Bartlett was 13 years old. Her funeral sermon, delivered by the Reverend Alexander Fletcher, was printed in Kingston, Ontario, and a copy of that text is preserved among the Bartlett Papers at the John Carter Brown Library. Smith Bartlett married his wife's older sister, Sarah Russell Gladding, a widow, on February 1, 1824. She died in Cape Vincent, New York, October 4, 1851, at age 71. The details are in John Russell Bartlett's, *Genealogy of That Branch of the Russell Family Which Comprises the Descendants of John Russell of Woburn, Massachusetts* (Providence: Providence Press Company, 1879), pp. 125–126.

2. According to Bartlett, his great-grandfather, Abner Bartlett, died in 1756, but Abner's wife, Abigail, "died in 1815, at the age of 104 years" (*Russell Genealogy*, 1879, p. 125). Also, Bartlett indicates his father's brothers and sisters are Anne, Phila, and Abner, but in the *Russell Genealogy* (p. 125), Smith Bartlett's siblings are listed as Anna, Alpha, Philadelphia, Mary, and Abner.

3. Nancy Russell's brothers and sisters are: Elizabeth, Jeremiah, John Newton, Martha, Amey (Amy), Mehitable, Sarah, and William (*Russell Genealogy*, 1879, pp. 35–37).

4. Kingston, Ontario, lies near the head of the St. Lawrence River, at the eastern end of Lake Ontario, approximately 90 miles southwest of Ottawa. Kingston's counterpart on the American side of the river is Cape Vincent, New York, about ten miles distant. Bartlett's father (Smith Bartlett) and several other mem-

bers of the Bartlett family lived in Cape Vincent during their later years.

5. According to Bartlett's *Russell Genealogy* (p.126), Smith Bartlett had already moved his family to Kingston, Ontario, in 1806.

6. Depending on the source consulted, this brief naval battle took place on November 9 or November 10, 1812, when Bartlett was seven years old, and his recollection of the events fifty-five years later were perhaps somewhat exaggerated by the passage of time. Apparently, Captain Isaac Chauncey of the U.S. Navy, in charge of the flagship *Oneida* and its attendant schooners stationed at Sackett's Harbor, New York, on the eastern end of Lake Ontario, lay in wait for the British ships to return from their operations further west, chasing the *Royal George* into the harbor at Kingston. The *Royal George* was assisted at the wharf by the militia that had been mobilized under Colonel John Vincent, while shore batteries near Kingston and at Point Henry kept the American ships largely at bay, although gunfire was exchanged that day until Captain Chauncey and his ships withdrew at dark. Owing to unfavorable wind conditions the next day, Chauncey and the American ships did not return to Kingston Harbor to reengage the *Royal George*. There was some damage inflicted on the vessels involved in the skirmish, and the Americans and the British each suffered one person killed and several injured. For a fuller account of the incident at Kingston, see J. Mackay Hitsman, *The Incredible War of 1812* (Toronto: University of Toronto Press, 1965), pp. 100–101, and John K. Mahon, *The War of 1812* (Gainesville: University of Florida Press, 1972), pp. 88–89.

7. Unless otherwise indicated, the following information on John Russell Bartlett's brothers and sisters is taken from the *Russell Genealogy* (pp. 127–142). Those individuals whose names are marked with a dagger (†), plus John Russell Bartlett's father (Smith Bartlett, Sr.) and stepmother (Sarah Russell Gladding Bartlett), are buried in St. John's Episcopal Cemetery in Cape Vincent.

William Russell Bartlett, born 1803. William was an employee of the Canadian government, having served nearly ten years each as a clerk in the offices of the Executive Council and the Governor-General, and for nearly twenty years, he was an Indian Commissioner in the Province of Ontario, working mostly among the Mohawk, Ojibwa, and Potawatomi tribes along the north shore of Lake Huron. Zachariah Allen of Providence, a long-time acquaintance of John Russell Bartlett, sent a copy of a monograph he had written, *Defence of the Rhode Island System of Treatment of the Indians, and of Civil and Religious Liberty* (Providence: Providence Press Company, 1876), to William Bartlett in 1877, and the latter made the contents of Allen's work known to the Canadian tribes and bands with whom he had worked. William Bartlett sent letters of appreciation from the Indians to Allen in the summer of 1877, including a long list of signatures and totems of the chiefs and other principal men of the tribes (MSS 254–Zachariah Allen Papers, Box 1, Folder 8, the Rhode Island Historical Society Library).

Smith Bartlett, Jr., born 1808. Smith lived most of his life in Belleville, Ontario, approximately fifty miles west of his hometown of Kingston. For many years he was in the mercantile business, but later in life he served quite successfully as Belleville's Police Magistrate or Judge of the Criminal Court. Smith Bartlett, Jr., died in 1868, and one of his sons, Clarence Russell Bartlett, died in 1877, leaving a wife, Cora, and a baby daughter. In a letter dated August 1, 1881, Cora writes to "Uncle" John Russell Bartlett, asking for money from relatives to help pay the cost ($70–$90) of a new brace for her daughter, now afflicted with a spinal condition. A note attached to her letter indicates Bartlett sent Cora $10 on August 11, 1881 (Bartlett Papers, John Carter Brown Library).

Martha Russell Bartlett†, born 1810. Martha was married to John Duvillard† of Cape Vincent, New York. Duvillard was a native of Geneva, Switzerland, where his father was the university president. The Duvillard's second son, John Antoine Duvillard†, married his first cousin, John Russell Bartlett's daughter, Anna. John Antoine Duvillard was a graduate of Yale and spent nearly the whole of the Civil War as an officer in the Army of the Potomac, dying a few days after the war's end in 1865. Sometime thereafter, Anna and her son, Henry Anthony Duvillard, moved to Providence, where they spent the rest of their lives.

George Francis Bartlett†, born 1812. George ran a mercantile business in New Orleans before he joined his brother, John Russell Bartlett, on the U. S. Boundary Commission in 1850. While serving as commissary on the commission, George was exonerated of a charge of having derived personal profit from the sale of government goods. Nevertheless, he was reassigned to another position on the commission, and the position of commissary was placed under military authority. George later ran a flour-milling operation in Cape Vincent, New York, where he also served as a Justice of the County Court and as acting Justice of the Peace.

Robert Coleman Bartlett†, born 1815. Robert also lived in Cape Vincent, New York, working in the mercantile business until his death at age thirty-eight.

8. According to *Lowville Academy: Semi-Centennial Anniversary Celebrated at Lowville, N.Y., July 21st and July 22d, 1858* (published in 1859 by the Lowville Home Committee), John Russell Bartlett is listed in 1819 as a student from New York City (p. 8), and Stephen W. Taylor, the popular principal mentioned by Bartlett, was hired by the academy in 1818 (p. 64).

9. Bartlett would have the opportunity to enjoy hunting again during the years he spent in the American Southwest as the U. S. Commissioner on the Mexican Boundary Survey, mostly as an occasional leisure activity, but at least once out of desperation. In September 1851, Bartlett was part of a small group that became lost in the lush bottomlands along Sonoita Creek a few miles downstream of modern-day Patagonia, Arizona. Reduced to eating a few fish from the creek and consuming boiled purslane, a

wild and edible plant common to the area, Bartlett hiked several miles northward into the Santa Rita Mountains, from which he returned to camp with a large turkey he had shot. His view from the Santa Rita Mountains, with Bartlett himself sitting in the foreground holding his gun, is captured in drawing number 180 in the Bartlett Collection at the John Carter Brown Library in Providence. That drawing, converted from a pencil field sketch by Bartlett to a shaded pencil and white by Oscar Bessau, has long carried the inexplicably erroneous title, *At Lost Camp, Texas*, although the topography in the scene, the dates on the verso of the drawing, and the evidence from Bartlett's field notes clearly place the commissioner at his "Lost Camp in southern Arizona" at the time.

10. The *Providence Directory* of 1828 lists William Russell's store and Bartlett's place of employment as 45 Westminster Street. Bartlett's residence at that time is listed as 101 Westminster, and William Russell's residence is given as 102 Westminster. The same address for William Russell's residence appears in Providence directories until the middle 1840s. The *Providence Directory* of 1830 indicates that Bartlett had moved his residence to 137 Westminster by that date, and William Russell had moved his business into room 25 of the Providence Arcade, also on Westminster Street. Care must be taken when considering these early Providence addresses, because the streets were subsequently renumbered.

According to the records of the Arcade Company, William Russell bought five shares in the Arcade on May 7, 1827, the year before the structure was built, and he acquired another ten shares on July 14, 1834. He apparently sold all of his Arcade shares in 1835, although for many years to come, he continued to operate his business in the building. See MSS 263–Arcade Company Records, the Rhode Island Historical Society Library.

11. The Providence Arcade has been a commercial icon in downtown Providence ever since its completion in 1828. Generally regarded as the oldest enclosed or indoor mall in the United States, the

three-story Arcade was designed in the Greek Revival style by architects Russell Warren and James Bucklin. The edifice, which extends from 65 Weybosset Street in the south to 130 Westminster Street in the north, is constructed of massive blocks of granite that were mined from the Bare Ledge Quarry in nearby Johnston, Rhode Island. Each of the porticos at the two ends of the Arcade is supported by six columns of granite, and each column is twenty-one feet high and weighs thirteen tons. Reportedly, the columns had to be dragged or skidded individually to the building site by a team of thirty oxen. Beyond the porticos and columns, a series of broad steps lead down to the streets. Inside, the Arcade is subdivided into dozens of small shops characteristic of the period in which it was built, and the large center court that runs the full length of the building receives abundant natural light through the glass roof. Narrow balconies on the upper two levels, constructed of hardwood floors and iron railings, overlook the spacious center court. Today, the Arcade is a National Historic Landmark, and the building is still occupied largely by specialty shops.

12. According to the *Providence Directory* of 1830 (p.146), the Bank of North America at that time was located at 26 Westminster Street.

13. Cyrus Butler's frugality would soon turn to philanthropy when he helped to endow the Butler Hospital for the Insane, a private facility now known simply as Butler Hospital. The hospital was established in 1844 along the old Pawtucket Road on the east side of Providence, at the modern address of 345 Blackstone Blvd. Major contributions for the establishment and maintenance of this hospital also came from Nicholas Brown, Jr., and his son, John Carter Brown. See Welcome Arnold Greene, *The Providence Plantations for Two Hundred and Fifty Years: An Historical Review of the Foundation, Rise, and Progress of the City of Providence* (Providence: J. A. & R. A. Reid, 1886), pp. 208–209.

14. In the manuscript, Bartlett initially wrote that he and Thomas
H. Webb were the founders of the Athenaeum, but later, he added
Frederick A. Farley's name to the sentence with a carat. Without
any further evidence or explanation for this addition, it would
be conjectural to assess whether Bartlett made the insertion as a
correction, or as a courtesy to Farley. However, the full participation of Farley in establishing the Athenaeum is documented
in Bartlett's own writing some twelve years later, for in his *Russell Genealogy* (1879, p. 129), Bartlett again credits himself as the
"original projector of the Providence Athenaeum. Calling in the
aid of the Rev. Dr. Frederick A. Farley and Dr. Thomas H. Webb,
they became the founders of this excellent institution, which now
possesses nearly fifty thousand volumes and has upwards of six
hundred members."

At the time the Athenaeum was established in 1831, Reverend
Farley, a graduate of Harvard, was the first minister of the Westminster Congregational Society, a Unitarian Church established
in 1828 in downtown Providence. Dr. Webb, a graduate of Brown
and Harvard, was a Providence physician who also served for several years as editor of the *Providence Journal*. Both men played
major roles in the development of the Athenaeum throughout
the decade of the 1830s. By 1841, both had moved from Providence—Farley to Brooklyn to head the Unitarian Congregational Church, and Webb to Boston for a career in journalism and
publishing, including a partnership in the firm of Marsh, Capen,
Lyon & Webb.

The precedent for a subscription library in Providence was set
seventy-eight years before Bartlett, Farley, and Webb made the
bold decision to establish the Providence Athenaeum. In 1753,
Stephen Hopkins, later a signer of the Declaration of Independence and a future governor of Rhode Island, and many members of the influential Brown family were among the original
subscribers to a new organization, the Providence Library Com-

pany. This library flourished for many decades, often under the leadership of the Browns, who also supported the institution financially. However, by the late 1820s, the library's well-worn and outdated collection of books no longer satisfied the needs of the local populace. This would have been especially true for the younger professionals who researched topics for public presentations in local philosophical organizations, including the Franklin Society, of which Bartlett, Farley, and Webb were members. For whatever reasons, the three men obviously decided to establish the Athenaeum rather than try to resurrect or reinvigorate the Providence Library Company. For more information on the history of the Providence Library Company, see Joseph LeRoy Harrison, "The Providence Athenaeum: 1753–1911," reprinted from the *New England Magazine*, September and October 1911, and Jane Lancaster, *Inquire Within* (Providence: Providence Athenaeum, 2003).

Further evidence of a loss of vitality in the Providence Library Company (PLC) comes from the organization's *Minute Book for the Providence Library*, a volume held by the current Athenaeum. It appears that the officers of the PLC held monthly meetings through the middle 1820s, but less frequently thereafter. On September 6, 1830, the PLC elected new officers for the following year. When those officers met on January 29, 1831, there was a quorum but no business, and the meeting was adjourned. Six weeks later, on April 14, 1831, the monthly meeting was adjourned for lack of a quorum. The stagnation in the PLC in the early 1830s is even more apparent when one looks at the organization's plan for the construction of its own building. Evidently, the Waterman family donated a lot on Benefit Street in Providence with the stipulation that the new library building must be constructed on that site within five years of the date of the gift. It appears the gift was made in 1830, although the PLC did not formally accept the offer until the library held its monthly business meeting on March 31, 1831. At one of the PLC's last meetings, on December

22, 1835, Zachariah Allen, in what must have been a most embarrassing moment for the officers, reported that the land offer from the Watermans had expired.

According to the records of the Providence Athenaeum, Bartlett was active in every aspect of the organization and operation of the new library. What follows is a chronology of Bartlett's documented participation during the first two years of the library's existence, based on manuscript material held in the archives of the Providence Athenaeum.

FEBRUARY 26, 1831. The earliest handwritten report, co-signed by John R. Bartlett, John Taylor, and Thomas H. Webb, is entitled, "Report of the Committee in Reference to the Projected Athenaeum." This report states that the Arcade has agreed to rent two rooms to the Athenaeum for a period of two years at a cost of $125.00 per year. It also describes how shares in the Athenaeum will sell for $25.00 each, with each share assigned one vote. Carpeting, shelves, cases, and all furniture for the new library are budgeted at $300.00. Annual expenses for rent, a keeper, and contingencies are estimated at $300.00 per year. The participation of John Taylor on this committee is significant because Taylor and Bartlett had been co-workers under Cyrus Butler at the Bank of North America. In addition, Taylor had been a long-time secretary and director of the Providence Library Company, thus providing Bartlett, Farley, and Webb with someone who had intimate knowledge of the recent history and operation of the Athenaeum's major competitor. All four men were among the original subscribers to the Athenaeum in 1831, with each holding a single $25.00 share.

JULY 18, 1831. The Providence Athenaeum elected its first set of officers and trustees. John Taylor was elected a Trustee. Frederick A. Farley was chosen 2nd Vice President, a position he also held in 1832. In 1833, Farley was advanced to 1st Vice President. Farley was also Library Director for the period 1834–1836.

Thomas H. Webb was elected Secretary in 1831, a position he also held in 1832. In 1834, Webb became 2nd Vice President. John R. Bartlett was chosen Treasurer in 1831, a position he held again in 1832. Much of the information on the trustees and officers of the Athenaeum, as well as a general history of the early Athenaeum, can be gleaned from the handwritten entries of meeting minutes and annual reports compiled in *Institution Records*, February 1831 – November 1835, an unpublished volume held by the Providence Athenaeum.

JULY 27, 1831. There are two committee reports from this date that are co-signed by Bartlett and Webb. These are from the committees on "Blank Books & Stationery" and "Purchase of Books."

AUGUST 10, 1831. "Report of Committee on Periodicals, etc.," signed by Webb and Bartlett. The Athenaeum has contracted with George Dana to buy several journals, including *American Quarterly, Edinburgh Quarterly Review, London Quarterly*, and *Southern Review*.

SEPTEMBER 5, 1831. Bartlett and Webb sign the reports from the "Committee on Regulations for Annual Subscribers" and the "Committee for Ascertaining Booksellers Terms"; a third report, from the "Committee on Fixing up the Rooms," is signed by Bartlett and William Butler.

SEPTEMBER 17, 1831. Letter from G & C & H Carvill to John Russell Bartlett. In response to Bartlett's request for book prices, the company writes, "it is a work of a great [deal] of trouble and labor to price a long list of single works. The list which you sent separately from the catalogue shall be marked and sent by mail this evening as we could not get it done in time for the Boat."

SEPTEMBER 19 and OCTOBER 3, 1831. A dual report from the "Library Committee" is signed by Bartlett and Webb.

NOVEMBER 28, 1831. Bartlett's Treasurer's Report.

Cash 14 patrons at $100 each	= 1400.00
Cash 68 shareholders at $25 each	= 1700.00
	3100.00
Paid:	
Furniture	= 297.16
Fixtures and Contingencies	= 114.78
Books	= 1304.76
Cash Balance	= $1383.30

NOVEMBER 28, 1831. "Report of Committee for Arranging the Library," signed by Webb, Farley, and Bartlett. "The Committee appointed to arrange the books and have catalogues of the same made out prepatory [preparatory] to the Library being opened for the use of the Members, have attended to their duty in as far as relates to classifying the works; an alphabetic catalogue is also in a state of forwardness, and the scientific one will be attended to with as little delay as possible."

JANUARY 2, 1832. "Report of Committee on Books Not to be Taken from the Library," signed by Bartlett and Webb.

MARCH 5, 1832. "Report of the Committee for Procuring a Librarian," signed by Webb and Bartlett. Daniel Cushing has been selected to serve as both Librarian and Keeper. His instructions for heating, lighting, and opening and closing the library are included in the report.

MAY 7, 1832. "Library Committee's Report in Reference to the Works Purchased at the Sale of the late William H. Elliott Esqr's Library," signed by Bartlett and Webb. The committee bought books and maps for $399.79, items that were estimated to have cost $967.49 elsewhere.

NOVEMBER 24, 1832. "Report on the State of the Library," signed by Farley, Webb, and Bartlett.

On July 5, 1832, the Providence Library Company appointed a "Committee of Conference" to discuss with the directors of the Athenaeum a possible merger of the two organizations. At approximately the same time, the Providence Athenaeum appointed its "Committee on the Subject of an Union with the Providence Library Company." Reports from both committees during the period 1832–1835, written by Zachariah Allen for the PLC and by Frederick Farley for the Athenaeum, indicate that little agreement could be reached on the proposed merger. Finally, a call was circulated to hold a meeting on January 25, 1836, to effect a union of the two libraries. Among the 59 signers of this call were: John Carter Brown, Nicholas Brown, Cyrus Butler, Moses B. Ives, Robert H. Ives, and Thomas H. Webb. It was agreed at the meeting to merge the two libraries into a newly chartered institution, to be called, "The Athenaeum." See William E. Foster, "The Providence Athenaeum," an unpublished and undated manuscript at the Providence Athenaeum.

When the "new" Athenaeum was chartered in 1836, Bartlett, Farley, and Webb were not only members and shareholders in the library, but they also served on the organization's first board of directors, along with Henry Anthony and John Carter Brown. Bartlett's share in the library, No. 279, was held in Bartlett's name until 1890; thereafter it passed to Bartlett's grandson, Henry Duvillard, whose wife, Margaret Duvillard, inherited the share in 1945. Bartlett's original share was reacquired by the Athenaeum in 1998. John Carter Brown and Nicholas Brown were also charter members of the new Athenaeum in 1836. See *The Providence Athenaeum: Charter, Constitution and By-Laws of the Athenaeum* (Providence: Knowles, Vose & Co., 1836), and "Proprietors: Providence Athenaeum," an unpublished ledger that lists each share and the history of its ownership from 1836 to the present. Both volumes are held in the Athenaeum's archives.

After the two libraries united in 1836 to form the Providence Athenaeum, it soon became apparent that the new library could no longer operate out of the cramped space the old Athenaeum had occupied at the Arcade. A permanent solution to the space problem came about when Nicholas Brown, Moses B. Ives, and Robert H. Ives donated land for the construction of a new Athenaeum building. This parcel of land, granted from the estate of Thomas P. Ives, is located at the corner of Benefit and College Streets, where the Athenaeum now stands. In addition to their magnanimous offer of land, the trio also agreed to donate $6,000.00 towards the construction of the new building and $4,000.00 towards the acquisition of new books, all contingent upon the Athenaeum's ability to raise matching funds. John Russell Bartlett and Henry Anthony were placed in charge of fund raising, and by the fall of 1836, the two had collected more than $15,000.00 in donations, including $1,000.00 each from Crawford Allen and Moses Brown, and $500.00 each from Zachariah Allen and Cyrus Butler. The Providence Athenaeum's new building, designed by the Philadelphia architect William Strickland, was completed in 1838 at a cost of just under $19,000.00 (see Fig. 2). See the *First Annual Report* of the Providence Athenaeum, February 27, 1837, and Jane Lancaster, *Inquire Within* (Providence: Providence Athenaeum, 2003), for detailed discussions of the gift of land and the ensuing construction and dedication of the new Providence Athenaeum building at 251 Benefit Street.

Bartlett continued to serve the Athenaeum long after his move to New York City in 1836. In addition to designing and decorating an Egyptian table in the late 1830s, Bartlett acquired many books for the Athenaeum. Sometimes Bartlett sold volumes directly to the Athenaeum from his Manhattan bookstore; at other times, he served as the Athenaeum's agent at auction sales in New York. After Bartlett returned to Providence permanently in the middle 1850s, and while serving as Rhode Island's Secretary of State, he again became very active in the affairs of the Athenaeum. He was on the library's board of directors from 1855 to 1858, and again in 1860, and for several of those years, he also served on the Library Committee. Bartlett is also given credit as the main writer of the Athenaeum's Annual Reports for the years 1856–1858.

15. *Description de l'Egypte: ou, Recueil des observations et des recherches qui ont été faites en Egypte pendant l'expédition de l'armee française* is a 23-volume set produced in Paris between 1808 and 1828. The subscribers to this work are listed as Messrs. Brown & Ives, Cyrus Butler, Amory Chapin, William G. Goddard, William Jenkins, H. N. Slater, Thomas J. Stead, and two anonymous. *Musée Français recueil des plus beaux tableaux, statues et bas-reliefs qui existaient au Louvre avant 1815, avec l'explication des subjets et discours sur la peinture, la sculpture, et la gravure*, also produced in Paris, is a 4-volume set that dates from 1803–1811. The *Musée Français* had six subscribers: William T. Grinnell, William W. Hoppin, William Jenkins, Amasa Manton, John Whipple, and one anonymous. *Le Musée royal: ou, Recueil de gravures d'apres les plus beaux tableaux, statues et bas-reliefs de la collection royale*, published in 1816–1818, is a 2-volume continuation of *Musée Français*. Bartlett, acting as an agent for the Athenaeum, bought all three of these large folio works in the late 1830s from London book dealer William C. Hall. Curiously, Bartlett does not mention the crown jewel of the Athenaeum's acquisitions, the double elephant folio edition of Audubon's *Birds of America*. This work was acquired in 1832 with funds supplied by twelve subscribers: John Russell Bartlett, Cyrus Butler, William Butler, Richard W. Greene, William T. Grinnell, Thomas C. Hoppin, John Kingsbury, John Mackie, Amasa Manton, Robert Rhodes, Samuel Shove, and Stephen Tripp. See *Third Annual Meeting of the Providence Athenaeum, September 24, 1838* (Providence: Knowles, Vose & Company, 1838), and Jane Lancaster, *Inquire Within*. The Audubon was sold at auction for the benefit of the Athenaeum's endowment in 2005.

16. The Egyptian table dates from ca. 1838 and is still utilized on the lower level of the current Providence Athenaeum. Measuring

approximately 5.5 × 9.0 feet, the enclosed table has a walnut rim and black canvas top; oversize drawers concealed behind double doors on the two ends; and a series of freestanding columns inset along the two longer sides. The colorful and detailed hieroglyphs applied by Bartlett are largely intact, although the base of the table is severely scuffed. Bartlett was not paid for his work on the cabinet, but the directors of the Athenaeum acknowledged his contribution as a "disinterested service in behalf of the Athenaeum, on the part of one of its early friends..." in their *5th Annual Report of the Providence Athenaeum*, September 25, 1840, p. 6. Cabinetmakers Millard and Lee of Williams Street in Providence were paid $102.50 on October 4, 1838, for constructing the table.

The following information is taken from, "A Temple for Tomes: The Egyptian Elephant Folio Cabinet in the Providence Athenaeum," by Christopher Monkhouse, *The Journal of Furniture History Society*, vol. xxvi, 1990, p. 160.

> Equally as striking as the table's temple form was the painted decoration on its surface. Although Bartlett had no specific temple in mind, an exact source for each decorative detail can be found in the *Description de l'Egypte*.... Because Bartlett was an accomplished artist in his own right, he was able to participate directly in this phase of the elephant folio cabinet's creation.... However, it should not be overlooked that Bartlett was assisted in decorating the cabinet by Kingsley (also spelt 'Kinsley') C. Gladding, a sign and ornamental painter.... According to the *Treasurer's Accounts*, Kingsley C. Gladding was paid by the Athenaeum $46.75 on 3 November 1840, for painting and varnishing the cabinet.

Another excellent source of information is Jean Brodahl, "John Russell Bartlett and the Egyptian Bookcase of the Providence Athenaeum," an unpublished manuscript on file at the Providence Athenaeum.

17. A & W Sprague Company was best known for its success in tex-

tile milling, especially as a producer of fine quality cotton and cal-
ico. Amasa Sprague was brutally murdered on New Year's Eve,
1843, at age forty-five, and the subsequent trial and execution
of his accused murderer caused a sensation in Rhode Island. His
brother, William Sprague III, had already been governor of Rhode
Island (1838–1839), and at the time of Amasa's death, William
was a U.S. Senator from the state. When William died in 1856,
his son, Byron, and Amasa's two sons, William Sprague IV and
Amasa, became partners in the A & W Sprague Manufacturing
Company. In 1861, William Sprague IV, on leave as Governor of
Rhode Island, became a celebrity for his heroism at the First Battle of Bull Run during the Civil War, with John Russell Bartlett,
his Secretary of State, serving as Acting Governor in Sprague's
absence. After William Sprague IV returned as governor, he had
a long career as a U.S. Senator beginning in 1863. The flamboy-
ant William Sprague married his first wife, Kate Chase, daughter of U.S. Secretary of the Treasury, Salmon P. Chase, in 1863,
and the Spragues proceeded to live an extravagant life style until
the eventual bankruptcy of the A & W Sprague Company in 1873.
For more on the Spragues and their company, see *Rhode Island: A
Guide to the Smallest State* (Boston: Houghton Mifflin Company,
1937), pp. 53–54; William G. McLoughlin, *Rhode Island: A Bicen-
tennial History* (New York: W. W. Norton & Company, 1978), pp.
166–168; and Peg A. Lamphier, *Kate Chase and William Sprague:
Politics and Gender in a Civil War Marriage* (Lincoln: University of
Nebraska Press, 2003).

18. It appears that John Russell Bartlett was an Episcopalian at
birth and at death, but on July 5, 1831, less than two months after
his marriage to Eliza Rhodes, he joined the Westminster Congregational Society (Unitarian Church) of his good friend and
associate, Reverend Frederick A. Farley. Church records indicate Bartlett remained a member until his move to New York
City several years later (MSS 134–Westminster Congregational
Society Records, the Rhode Island Historical Society Library).

Also, according to the *Providence Directory* of 1832, the Globe Bank, above which John and Eliza lived, was at that time located at 52 South Main Street.

19. Bartlett produced many drawings and paintings during his lifetime. He worked in pencil, ink, sepia and wash, watercolor, and oil. The oldest known work by Bartlett is a signed and dated sepia and wash from 1828 that depicts Barre, the famous dog that rescued snow-bound travelers near the Convent of St. Bernard in Switzerland (see Fig. 21). This drawing displays intricate detail of the young boy carried on the dog's back, the hair on the dog, and the rope or cord around the dog's neck, from which a leather bottle or flask is suspended. Below the drawing is a text, written in Bartlett's calligraphic hand, which describes Barre and his exploits. Bartlett entered *Barre* and two other drawings, one of a cake and the other of a shipwrecked mariner, in a Providence exhibition on August 1, 1829 (William H. Gerdts and James Yarnell, *Index to American Art Exhibition Catalogues* [Boston: G. K. Hall, 1986], p. 192). The ownership of the Barre drawing after 1829 and before 1899 is not known, but in the latter year, *Barre* was given as a wedding present to a young couple in Providence. *Barre* is still owned by descendents of that family, although the drawing no longer resides in Rhode Island. The fate of the drawings of the cake and the shipwrecked mariner is not known.

Bartlett's most famous painting, *The Great September Gale of 1815*, hangs in a Rhode Island Historical Society building in Providence, the Aldrich House (see Fig. 22). The *Great Gale*, a bequest to the society by Bartlett in 1886, is an oil on canvas that measures approximately 32 x 41". It depicts the hurricane of September 23, 1815, that brought record flooding and destruction to what are now downtown Providence and the waterfront at the mouth of the Providence River. Although the painting is unsigned and undated, it almost certainly dates from the 1830s, the decade immediately prior to Bartlett's becoming established as a bookdealer in New York City. Bartlett's rendition of this

FIGURE 21

The Dog Barre of the Convent of St Bernard, a sepia and wash, signed and dated, "John R. Bartlett. 1828." This is the oldest known surviving work by Bartlett and is one of a set of three drawings he entered in an art exhibition in Providence in 1829. The elaborately written text below the drawing reads,

"At the Convent of St Bernard in Switzerland. Dogs are trained to go in search of travellers, who have lost their way in traversing the Alps. The Dog Barre in his excursions among the mountains and Glaciers, has saved the lives of upwards of 40 unfortunate travellers, by their partaking of the Cordial (that he always carried in a leather Bottle suspended to his neck) and afterwards conducting them safely to the Convent. Recently, in one of his hospitable excursions, he found a child asleep and almost frozen in a Cavern of Ice, in the celebrated Glacier of Balsore [?], his parents having perished by an avalanche. Barry by his caresses, animated the child, got him mounted on his back and carried him safely to the Convent. The skin of this dog is now preserved with his Collar & Bottle, and stands in the Museum of Berne."

This drawing has descended through a prominent Rhode Island family since 1899 and is reproduced here through the generosity of David W. Love and Jane Matteson Love.

The Dog Barrè of the Convent of St Bernard.

FIGURE 21

FIGURE 22

The Great Gale of September 1815, ca. 1835, an oil painting by John Russell Bartlett. Among the surviving pieces of artwork by Bartlett, the *Great Gale* is both the largest work and his only known oil painting. Bartlett's version of the Great Gale is similar to the one painted by James Kidder of Boston in 1815; that oil was released as a print the following year under the title, *A Representation of the Great Storm at Providence, Sept. 23rd 1815*. Given that Henry Cheever Pratt also produced a painting of the Great Gale at approximately the same time that Bartlett produced his, it is possible that Bartlett's decision to produce the *Great Gale* was influenced more by Pratt than by Kidder. In all of these versions of the Great Gale, the view is to the west, looking across the windswept surface of the Providence River, into the flooded commercial district of downtown Providence.

The following quotation is taken from Robert P. Emlen, "The Great Gale of 1815: Artifactual Evidence of Rhode Island's First Hurricane," *Rhode Island History*, vol. 48, no. 2, May 1990, pp. 51–60. Although Emlen is describing the scene in Kidder's print, the same narrative applies to Bartlett's oil painting.

"None of the buildings represented in Kidder's print are standing today. They were well known at the time, however, and the scene was immediately recognizable to the contemporary public. At the left of the print are commercial buildings on what is now the corner of Dyer and Westminster streets. At the center, across Westminster Street, is the Washington Insurance Company, on the current site of the Hospital Trust Building. . . . Kidder's view must therefore have been made from the eastern end of the Weybosset Bridge, likely from an upper floor of the Brick Market House. . . . In Kidder's print the river is surging up into the Cove at the right. The old Weybosset Bridge has vanished without a trace."

In Bartlett's rendition of the Great Gale, the scene is even more chaotic than in Kidder's, especially his characterization of the storm waves and the amount and types of debris carried by the wind. Courtesy of the Rhode Island Historical Society. Rhi x3 3078.

FIGURE 22

FIGURE 23

Sculptured Rocks near the Gila is a combination of pencil, white ink, and sepia and wash that Bartlett employed to show examples of rock art along the Gila River. The examples he depicts were sketched on June 21, 1852, at a site on the north end of Antelope Hill, between Yuma and Gila Bend, Arizona. According to Bartlett,

"Towards evening, when the sun began to lose its force, I took my sketch-book and went to the base of the bluff, where I had noticed as we passed a number of inscribed rocks. I found hundreds of these boulders covered with rude figures of men, animals, and other objects of grotesque forms, all pecked in with a sharp instrument.... One draws an animal such as he sees; another makes one according to his own fancy; and a third amuses himself with devising grotesque or unmeaning figures of other sorts. Hence we find these sculptured rocks in large numbers in prominent places." (1854, *Personal Narrative*, vol. 2, pp. 195–196).

This drawing is number 154 in the Bartlett Collection at the John Carter Brown Library.

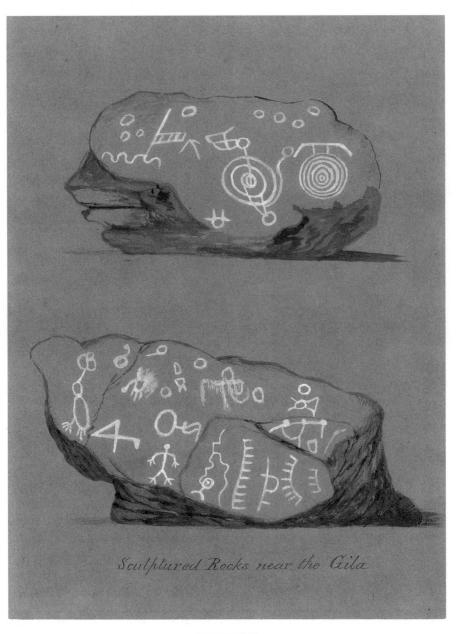

Sculptured Rocks near the Gila

FIGURE 23

FIGURE 24

Guadalupe Pass, on Cooke's Road—Sonora, a sepia and wash dated August 4, 1852, is drawing number 41 in the Bartlett Collection at the John Carter Brown Library. Cooke's Road is a famous wagon trail that was constructed in 1846 by Colonel St. George Cooke and his Mormon Battalion on their march to California during the Mexican-American War. This portion of the trail is on the Cloverdale Ranch in extreme southwestern New Mexico, and the view is to the southwest. Bartlett describes this scene in his *Personal Narrative* (1854, vol. 2, pp. 330–331):

"The worst is a chalky hill, near the last in the pass.... To ascend this place with loaded wagons, is impossible.... The contents were put upon the backs of the mules, which were sent ahead again to deposit their loads. We then took hold of the wagons; and by alternately pushing them and chocking the wheels, the mules got them up this formidable ascent with comparative ease. While this was going on I took a sketch of the pass...."

FIGURE 25

Residence of Joseph W. Osborne Esq. Napa Valley, a pencil sketch made by John R. Bartlett on March 25, 1852. Joseph Osborne was a San Francisco merchant and Napa Valley farmer who accompanied Bartlett and several others on a trip to the geysers of northern California in late March 1852. Osborne's principal residence, Oak Knoll Farm, is shown in this scene, as is the full width of Napa Valley and the mountains beyond, including Mount George on the far skyline. Bartlett was impressed with the fact Osborne had accomplished so much with his farm in the space of a year, having hired New England farmhands, including several from Bartlett's home state of Rhode Island, who brought the virgin valley land into cultivation, built redwood fences, and planted a great variety of crops. The Osborne house, which Bartlett described as being in the style of a New England cottage (1854, *Personal Narrative*, vol. 2, p. 16), has been remodeled and enlarged several times since Bartlett's visit in 1852. It now resembles a large southern mansion, complete with tall columns and verandas on the exterior, surrounded by flower gardens and trees, some of the latter upwards of 150 feet tall. This drawing is number 171e in the Bartlett Collection at the John Carter Brown Library.

FIGURE 26

This watercolor, entitled *Casa Grandes, near the River Gila—Arizona*, is drawing number 10 in the Bartlett Collection held by the John Carter Brown Library. It is based on a pencil field sketch Bartlett made on July 12, 1852, when he was U.S. Boundary Commissioner in the American Southwest. The view is to the northeast across a site that is preserved today as Casa Grande Ruins National Monument near Coolidge, Arizona. Casa Grande is an extensive array of Hohokam adobe structures that were built south of the Gila River some time prior to A.D. 1400. The major structure in this scene is a four-story Great House; its walls are constructed of successive courses of caliche mud. Casa Grande today looks much the way Bartlett saw it in 1852, although more of the main structure and portions of the surrounding walls have crumbled since his visit.

FIGURE 27

Squantum from the Bridge, a watercolor by John Russell Bartlett, ca. 1880. Another title or statement on the verso reads, "Squantum from the Bridge leading to Huckleberry Island." This is one of the better watercolors by Bartlett, taken from a collection of twenty-six of his drawings owned by the Rhode Island Historical Society. Squantum is located on an island on the east side of the Providence River, near Squantum Woods State Park in East Providence. It was founded as an all-male retreat and dinner club in 1872, with its name probably taken from the Squantum feasts, especially those of seafood, that were common in New England among the Native Americans and colonists. Squantum still operates as an association that hosts private dinners for special occasions. The small but steep island on the left is Squantum Point, located at 41° 47' 19" N. Lat., 71° 22' 23" W. Long. The facilities of the club are located on the larger island shown in the right-center of Bartlett's scene. Today, a railroad track and bike path run along the right side of the larger island. The view is to the northwest. Courtesy of the Rhode Island Historical Society. Rhi X3 5254.

FIGURE 28

Old Stone Mill. Newport is another watercolor done by John Russell Bartlett late in his career, probably ca. 1880. Located in Touro Park in Newport and open to the public, the Old Stone Mill, sometimes referred to as the Newport Tower, is a structure whose origin and function are not entirely agreed upon by the experts who have examined it, although most authorities believe it to be the relic of a former windmill from the very early colonial period. Others believe the mill is older and likely the product of early Norse or Portuguese voyages. The circular mill has an outside diameter of 23 feet and stands 24.5 feet high; a series of eight Romanesque arches rise 7.5 feet above its base. The mill is constructed of slate, stones, and mortar derived from local sources (Manuel Luciano DaSilva, "Portuguese Tower of Newport," in *Portuguese Pilgrims & Dighton Rock* [Bristol, Rhode Island, 1971], pp. 74–78). Courtesy of the Rhode Island Historical Society. Rhi X3 5257.

catastrophe is not based on any first-hand knowledge, since he was just nine years old and living in Canada at the time of the storm. He appears to have copied the scene from an oil painting produced by James Kidder of Boston in ca. 1815, a work that Kidder issued as a print the following year. In 1974, Bartlett's *Great Gale* formed part of an exhibition, "American Narrative Painting," held at the Los Angeles County Museum of Art. Related to this exhibition, there is a good discussion of the provenance of the Bartlett painting in a letter to Albert T. Klyberg from Donelson F. Hoopes, dated August 25, 1975, in the RIHS records.

It is intriguing that Henry Cheever Pratt (1803–1880), another Boston artist and a long-time acquaintance of Bartlett, also produced an oil painting of the Great Gale in the 1830s. According to Robert P. Emlen's "The Great Gale of 1815: Artifactual Evidence of Rhode Island's First Hurricane" (*Rhode Island History*, vol. 48, May, 1990, p. 58), Pratt announced in 1835 that his rendition of the painting was available for public viewing at a charge of twenty-five cents. In all likelihood, Pratt's association with Bartlett dates back to the middle 1820s when the two young men lived and worked in Providence. Therefore, it may be more than a coincidence that Bartlett and Pratt produced their oil paintings of the Great Gale at approximately the same time.

The largest collection of Bartlett artwork is found in the John Carter Brown Library in Providence. This collection totals approximately 235 drawings in pencil, ink, sepia and wash, and watercolor, with some 175 to 200 pieces created by Bartlett himself. The rest of the drawings in this collection are by artists associated with Bartlett: Oscar Bessau, Henry B. Brown, Harrison Eastman, and Henry Cheever Pratt. Nearly all of the drawings in the collection are associated with Bartlett's tenure as Boundary Commissioner in the Southwest from 1850 to 1853. For most of this period, from the summer of 1851 to the spring of 1853, Henry Pratt was an official draughtsman and field artist on the survey, accompanying Bartlett through vast areas of New Mexico, Arizona, California, Sonora, and Chihuahua. In recent years, one of Pratt's rare sketchbooks, dating from the spring and summer of 1852 and containing fifty-some drawings, was purchased by an astute individual at a California sale.

In addition to his work for the Boundary Commission, Pratt was allowed to paint part-time for private individuals in order to supplement his income. In 2002, I identified an oil painting of a government encampment at Old Town, San Diego, as a Pratt painting. The scene shows several government personnel and a series of tents located along the San Diego River, with an extended oblique view up and across Mission Valley in the distance. Alexander M. Harrison (1829–1881) of the United States Coast Survey, which in the early 1850s was mapping the coast of California, had commissioned the San Diego painting from Pratt for $25.00. In addition to the works Pratt produced while on the Boundary Commission, he converted many of his Southwestern scenes into large oil paintings after his return to Boston in 1853. Those paintings of his that survive have become quite valuable. For example, Pratt's painting of the Copper Mines of southern New Mexico sold at auction in November 2002 for $59,750.

Another thirteen watercolors from the Boundary Commission period were painted by Seth Eastman in 1853 at Bartlett's request. The Eastman watercolors were donated anonymously to the Rhode Island School of Design in the late 1940s, and then transferred to the John Carter Brown Library to become part of the Bartlett Collection. In 1994, however, the watercolors were returned to the Rhode Island School of Design and now reside in the RISD Museum of Art in Providence, almost directly across the street from the site of Bartlett's residence on Benefit Street from 1865 to 1886. Eastman was a West Point graduate and an army artist who is best known for his memorable scenes of the Indians of the northern Great Plains. Eastman's wife, Mary, published extensively on the American Indian and incorporated many of her husband's drawings into her books. According to letters housed in the Bartlett Papers at the John Carter Brown Library, the Eastmans reminded Bartlett on more than one occasion that he needed to forward funds sufficient to pay for the thirteen watercolors. In spite of this debt, however, the correspondence between Bartlett and the Eastmans was always cordial. See M. Eastman to J. R. Bartlett, September 18, 1855, October 1, 1855, and April 3, 1856; and S. Eastman to J. R. Bartlett, August 27, 1853 and October 8, 1855, all in the Bartlett Papers.

There are three excellent sources of information on the drawings in the Bartlett Collection. *Bartlett's West*, by Robert V. Hine, (New Haven: Yale University Press, 1968), is the earliest work and includes forty-eight full-page color reproductions of sepia and washes and watercolors. *Drawing the Borderline*, edited by Dawn Hall (Albuquerque: Albuquerque Museum, 1996), includes more of the Bartlett drawings than *Bartlett's West*, and in addition to the large color reproductions, there are many smaller black and whites. Two chapters in this volume, "Drawing Borders: Art and the Cultural Politics of the U.S.-Mexico Boundary Survey 1850–1853," pp. 23–77, by Gray Sweeney, and "Artist Collaborators: A Surrogate Hand—Seth Eastman's for Bartlett's," pp. 79–94, by Lucretia Hoover Giese, are especially useful. For a more complete description of the Bartlett drawings and the field sites at which the original sketches were taken, see *An Annotated Guide to the Artwork of the United States Boundary Commission, 1850–1853*, by Jerry E. Mueller (Las Cruces, New Mexico: GEM Enterprises, 2000). This source describes every drawing in the Bartlett Collection, as well as the Eastman watercolors, and more than 120 scenes are reproduced in black and white. In addition, there are tables in the guide that crosslist the drawings in the Bartlett Collection with those Bartlett published in his *Personal Narrative* in 1854. Also in this work, I have identified, more precisely than had ever been done before, the locations of the field sites at which the scenes were depicted by John Russell Bartlett and others.

20. During this stage of his life, Bartlett was a partner and officer in the Providence Exploring Company, which sent a ship to the coast of West Africa to ascend and explore the Niger River in quest of a great number of goods, the top ten in order being: gold dust, ivory, indigo, ostrich plumes, skins of wild animals, gum arabic, bullock hides, honey, palm oil, and camwood and barwood. Other partners in this venture included Richard A. Arnold, Daniel Greene, and Elijah Pierce. There is no evidence of financial success by this company, and, "The Seamen's Accounts attest that there was a fearful mortality among them while they were trading off the African Coast." See John Russell Bartlett, *Letter of Instructions to the Captain and the Supercargo of the Brig 'Agenoria,'—Engaged in a Trading Voyage to Africa; Letter of Instructions—Inventory of Merchandise and Seamen's Accounts; A Merchant Venture Overseas by the Providence Exploring Company*, privately printed for Howard Greene (Milwaukee) and Arnold G. Talbot (Philadelphia), 1933. The impetus for Bartlett's involvement in shipping and exploration probably came from his former employer at the Bank of North America, Cyrus Butler, who himself had been a partner with Edward Carrington & Company in the *Mercury* and *Superior*, two vessels which operated along the coast of South America during the 1820s (see MSS 558–Henry Mathewson Papers, Rhode Island Historical Society Library).

21. Bartlett does not appear to have been actively involved in the Providence Franklin Society until after he started working in the Providence banks in the late 1820s. This assertion is in part supported by the fact that his name does not appear on the society's membership lists for the years 1823–1826. Bartlett's name, however, does appear on an undated Franklin Society membership list that follows the organization's 1832 charter. Also on that list are the names of several of Bartlett's closest associates: Henry Anthony, Fred A. Farley, William Grinnell, William W. Hoppin, Thomas P. Ives, Seth Padelford, and Thomas H. Webb. According to a record book of donations made to the Franklin Society,

Bartlett contributed a lithographic stone from Upper Canada on September 20, 1831, and among his other donations are a salamander and several coins and medals. Apparently, Bartlett's younger brother, George F. Bartlett, donated a group of "Indian Relics" to the society on January 29, 1833 (MSS 162–Providence Franklin Society Records, Folders 1 and 8, the Rhode Island Historical Society Library).

Of the papers Bartlett read before the Franklin Society, at least two handwritten manuscripts are preserved at the John Carter Brown Library (Bartlett Papers, Box 13, Miscellaneous Papers). One paper of 40 pages was read November 27, 1833, and is entitled, "On the varieties of the Human Race." A second manuscript of 22 pages, entitled, "On the Indian Languages," was read in February 1836. Thus, Bartlett's interest in ethnology was already firmly established during his younger years in Providence and would ultimately lead to his co-founding of the American Ethnological Society in New York less than a decade later. His particular interest in Indian languages would also prompt Bartlett to collect numerous vocabularies during the early 1850s, a period in which he served as Boundary Commissioner in the American Southwest. These original vocabularies, mostly assembled by Bartlett from interviews he conducted in the field, survive in the collections at the John Carter Brown Library and the National Anthropological Archives of the Smithsonian Institution. Included among the vocabularies are the Cahita, Chumash, Cochimi, Comanche, Diegueño, Kiliwa, Kiowa, Luiseño, Maricopa, Mimbreno Apache, Opata, Pima, Seri, Tarahumara, Tiwa-Piro, Yuma, and Yaqui culture groups. Many of these Indian languages were cited and/or published by other authors during Bartlett's lifetime, and at least one of his vocabularies, "The Language of the Piro," was published posthumously by Frederick Webb Hodge in the *American Anthropologist*, 1909, pp. 426–433.

22. Dighton Rock is a 40-ton sandstone boulder that is polished smooth on its top, but is elsewhere weathered, oxidized, and

rough to the touch. Transported and dumped by Ice Age glaciers, the boulder came to rest near the head of the estuary of the Taunton River between Fall River and Taunton, Massachusetts, with only its top protruding above the water line. On that portion of the rock that faces outwardly toward the open water, a great series of figures are carved or scratched into the surface of the rock, and the origin of these markings has been debated for centuries. In addition to the attribution to the Norse by Carl Christian Rafn and others, there have been leading proponents of a Portuguese origin in the sixteenth century, including Edmund B. Delabarre and Manuel L. da Silva. In recent times, the rock has been elevated eleven feet to raise it above high water level, and it now forms part of a permanent exhibit, encased in glass, all within an octagonal building designated as the "Dighton Rock Museum" in Dighton Rock State Park. See Manuel L. da Silva, *Portuguese Pilgrims and Dighton Rock* (Bristol, Rhode Island, 1971); Edmund B. Delabarre, *Dighton Rock: A Study of the Written Rocks of New England* (New York: Walter Neale, 1928); and Carl C. Rafn, *Antiquitates Americanae: Scriptores septentrionales rerum Ante-Columbianarum in America* (Copenhagen, Denmark, 1837).

23. Albert Gallatin (1761–1849), born and educated in Switzerland, had a highly eclectic and successful career as a politician, statesman, diplomat, and banker. Although he is best known for his role as Secretary of the Treasury for thirteen years (1801–1814) under Thomas Jefferson and James Madison, Gallatin also maintained interests in history, ethnology, and international diplomacy, and among these varied subjects, he published a great many essays. For a biography of Gallatin, see John Austin Stevens, *Albert Gallatin*, the American Statesmen series, Volume XIII (Boston and New York: Houghton Mifflin, 1899), and Ray Walters, Jr., *Albert Gallatin: Jeffersonian Financier and Diplomat* (New York: Macmillan, 1957).

24. Bartlett indicates he entered the book business with Charles Welford in New York City in either 1840 or 1841. The actual

NOTES FOR PAGES 24–26

year must have been 1840, because there is a letter from Charles
Henry of Savannah, dated July 20, 1840, in which Henry states he
has received the "catalog of books for sale by Bartlett & Welford"
(Bartlett Papers, John Carter Brown Library).

There are two printed catalogues at the John Carter Brown
Library from the early years of Bartlett & Welford's bookstore.
The older is dated 1841 and carries the title, *Catalogue of Books,
Ancient and Modern, in Every Department of Literature and Science,
For Sale by Bartlett & Welford, Booksellers and Importers of English
Books at their Antiquarian Bookstore, and Repository for Standard Lit-
erature*, at "229 Broadway, under the American Hotel." This catalogue carries an incredible 3,363 entries arranged alphabetically
by author. Among the items for sale are: five works by Sir Walter
Scott; many volumes on Shakespeare; and a complete set of 168
volumes of the *Gentleman's Magazine* from the period 1731–1838
available for $250.00. Three years later, in 1844, another cata-
logue was issued of 116 pages and carries the title, *Catalogue of an
Extensive Collection of Theological Books, Ancient and Modern, Including English and Foreign Editions, Comprising a Choice Selection of Rare
and Standard Works in Theology and Divinity, Biblical Literature, Eccle-
siastical History, Writings of the Old English Divines, Etc., Now for Sale
at the Low Prices Affixed to Each Article, for Cash, by Bartlett & Welford, Antiquarian Bookstore and Repository for Standard Literature, No.
7 Astor House, Broadway, New York*. This catalogue was originally
printed in three parts: "Part 1. Theology" has 1,352 entries; "Part
2. American History" has entries 1401–2832; and "Part 3. General
Literature" has entries 2833–6606.

25. Bartlett was the first Corresponding Secretary of the American
Ethnological Society, a position he held through the late 1840s.
In a two-page biographical sketch of Bartlett that appears to have
been written in early 1878, Henry Drowne, Bartlett's cousin, indicates that many meetings of the AES during its early years were
held at Bartlett's house, No. 1 Amity Street in New York City. Of
the several copies of this publication held by the Providence Ath-

enaeum, one contains an original letter from Drowne to Bartlett dated March 1, 1878. According to Drowne, "At the last meeting of the American Ethnological Society Mr. Benj. G. Arnold placed the engraving of you (framed) in a prominent place in his parlor where all could see it upon entering the room." See "John Russell Bartlett," *The American Portrait Gallery, with Biographical Studies,* edited by Lillian C. Buttre (New York: J. C. Buttre, 1880). Also featured in this book are Henry B. Anthony, George Bancroft, Nicholas Brown, Ambrose Burnside, Bishop Thomas Clark, Esek Hopkins, and Francis Wayland.

The AES during its early years under Bartlett and Gallatin included many fields of inquiry: archeology, anthropology, geography, history, literature, travel, etc. Therefore, it is not surprising to find that its early membership, largely confined to the New York City area, was made up of a mix of practicing professionals, among whom virtually none were specialists in the field of ethnology. Later in the nineteenth century, as specialization by and within disciplines became commonplace, the AES survived by narrowing its focus to studies that are based in what would now be called socio-cultural anthropology. In the twentieth century, the AES became a national and international organization, and today it boasts a membership of approximately 4,000 anthropologists. Although now a section within the American Anthropological Society, the AES has its own officers separate from the AAS and publishes its own journal, *American Ethnologist.*

26. At the head of this paragraph on the original manuscript is a note Bartlett inserted in pencil, "First meeting, Nov. 19/42," i.e., November 19, 1842.

27. The two major publications by Gallatin on these subjects are: *Thoughts on the Proposed Annexation of Texas to the United States* (New York: S. W. Benedict & Co., 1844), 2nd edition, and *Peace with Mexico* (New York: Bartlett & Welford, 1847). Given Bartlett's involvement with Gallatin, and the fact that he helped write and publish the latter essay, it is somewhat surprising that Bartlett

did not meet with more resistance from southerners when the full Senate considered his nomination for U.S. Boundary Commissioner in 1850. Bartlett's personal copy of *Peace with Mexico*, with notes, letters, and clippings, is found in Box 1, Folder 12 of MSS 286–John Russell Bartlett Papers, Rhode Island Historical Society Library.

28. There is a long-standing and controversial legend about North America having been discovered in A.D. 1170 by Prince Madoc of Wales. Much has been written about the supposed entry of Madoc's ships into Mobile Bay and the subsequent settlements of the Welsh in various parts of the Mississippi River Basin. The interaction of the Welsh with the Native Americans is purported to have produced light-skinned Indians who spoke a Welsh-like language—the Mandans, whose numbers were subsequently decimated by smallpox. Bartlett's unpublished manuscript, "Essay on the claim of the Welsh with Discovery of America in the 10th Century," ca. 1847, is held by the John Carter Brown Library. Although originally a book-length treatise, approximately half of the original text has been lost. Bartlett added a handwritten note to his essay to help explain the missing sections: "These chapters were lent to Dr. Hawks and by him given to a Mr. Jones connected with a Welsh newspaper in Utica in the year 1857 or so—and never returned to me. Mr. Jones promised to translate and publish the essay." The reference here is to the Reverend Francis Lister Hawks, an Episcopalian clergyman and author in New York City. Hawks apparently borrowed rather freely from Bartlett's material, since there is a note from the 1850s that indicates Hawks also borrowed eight of the Indian vocabularies that Bartlett had collected in the American Southwest (Bartlett Papers, Box 13, Miscellaneous Papers, John Carter Brown Library). Some of these vocabularies might be lost as well.

The following material from the Madoc manuscript has survived, including several chapter sleeves. In addition, there are several pages of manuscript related to Madoc that are found in

Box 13 (Loose Papers) of the Bartlett Papers at the John Carter Brown Library.

Two untitled sections with pages numbered 1–16 and 13–22½, respectively. Bartlett quotes the *Gentleman's Magazine*, vol. 10, 1740.

Chapter 3, no title, pages 92–108. The chapter sleeve carries the title, "Connection between the Welsh & Scandinavians."

Chapter 4, "Accounts of Welsh and White People among the Aborigines of America," pages 109–150, with a few of the pages written on the back of blank ledger paper from Jessup & Swift Company. The single sleeve marked for chapters 4 & 5 is titled, "Accounts of Welsh and White Indians in America." Therefore, it is possible this long section of manuscript includes material Bartlett intended for chapter 5.

Chapter 5, missing, or largely incorporated into chapter 4.

Chapter 6, "Remains of an Ancient People in Tennessee, Kentucky, Missouri and the parts adjacent," pages 165–201. The title of the chapter sleeve is, "Remains of an ancient people in Tennessee, Kentucky & Missouri—and traditions of the Indians respecting such a race."

Chapter 7, "Relics of a Civilized Race in the Western States," title page, only.

Chapter 8, "Examination & Comparison of the foregoing evidence," pages 227–265½. The chapter sleeve carries the title, "Recapitulation and critical examination of the several accounts."

Chapter 9, "Objections to the pretensions of the Welsh," title page (page 244), only. The chapter sleeve carries the same title.

The overlapping pagination in the introductory chapter and the dual titles for some of the other chapters suggest Bartlett expanded and revised his manuscript over a period of years. Although the manuscript at the John Carter Brown Library is listed as ca. 1847, there is evidence to suggest a portion of the writing was completed much earlier. For example, in a letter dated April 4, 1839, at a time when Bartlett was very active in the reinvigorated New-York Historical Society, John Russell indicates he met a fellow from St. Louis who had attended Bartlett's lecture on Madoc in New York City. Also, there are several other letters to Bartlett about Madoc that date from the same period (Bartlett Papers, John Carter Brown Library). Thus, it appears Bartlett wrote some of his text already in the late 1830s when he was still associated with the firm of Jessup & Swift. That a number of his manuscript pages are written on the company's ledger paper strengthens the probability that Bartlett's initial work on Madoc predates 1847.

It is possible that Bartlett's interest in Madoc was inspired by, *The Welch Indians; or, A collection of papers, respecting a people whose ancestors emigrated from Wales to America, in the year 1170, with Prince Madoc, (three hundred years before the first voyage of Columbus), and who are said now to inhabit a beautiful country on the west side of the Mississippi*, extracts from the *Gentleman's Magazine* (1789–1792) and correspondence, printed for T. Chapman, London, 1797 [?]. Also, Bartlett would have had access to the individual Madoc articles from the complete set of the *Gentleman's Magazine* that Bartlett & Welford had for sale in their catalogue of 1841. The debate surrounding Madoc's putative visit to North America continued long after Bartlett's interest in the subject waxed in the 1840s and 1850s. For a more recent account, see Richard Deacon, *Madoc and the Discovery of America: Some new light on an old controversy* (New York: G. Braziller, 1967), and Gwyn A. Williams, *Madoc, The Making of a Myth* (London: Eyre Methuen, 1979).

29. Frédéric de Waldeck, *Voyage pittoresque et archéologique dans la province Yucatan (Amérique Centrale), pendant les années 1834 et 1836* (Paris: B. Dufour et Co., 1838).

30. John L. Stephens, *Incidents of Travel in Central America, Chiapas, and Yucatan* (New York: Harper and Brothers, 1841), 2 volumes.

31. Tumuli is plural for tumulus, a type of ancient sepulchral mound. These mounds are usually constructed of earth or stones piled on top of a grave.

32. Ephraim George Squier and Edwin Hamilton Davis, *Ancient Monuments of the Mississippi Valley: Comprising the Results of Extensive Original Surveys and Explorations* (Washington, D.C.: Smithsonian Institution, Contributions to Knowledge, vol. 1, 1848). A slightly earlier treatment of this subject is, "Observations on the aboriginal monuments of the Mississippi Valley; the character of the ancient earth-works, and the structure, contents, and purposes of the mounds; with notices of the minor remains of ancient art. With illustrations," from the second volume of the *Transactions of the American Ethnological Society* (New York: Bartlett & Welford, 1847).

33. Two major publications by E. G. Squier are: *Notes on Central America; Particularly the States of Honduras and San Salvador: Their Geography, Topography, Climate, Population, Resources, Productions, etc., etc., and the Proposed Honduras Inter-oceanic Railway* (New York: Harper & Brothers, 1855), and *Nicaragua; Its People, Scenery, Monuments, Resources, Condition, and Proposed Canal* (New York: Harper & Brothers, revised edition, 1860).

34. *Dictionary of Americanisms* was Bartlett's greatest commercial writing success. First published in 1848, it was revised and enlarged through three succeeding editions—1859, 1861, and 1877—and published by Little, Brown & Company in Boston. In December 2002, John Wiley & Sons issued a facsimile reproduction of the first edition of 1848, promoting the book as "A rediscovered classic."

35. John B. Weller (1812–1875), a Democrat originally from Ohio, was appointed in 1849 by outgoing President James Polk to run the boundary line between the United States and Mexico. The incoming Whig administration of Zachary Taylor was upset at

Polk's last-minute appointment of Weller, especially Taylor's Secretary of the Interior, Thomas Ewing, who was also from Ohio and who had long been a political adversary of Weller. Weller was removed as Boundary Commissioner in California in early 1850 for reasons of internal dissension and fiscal mismanagement. Weller also had the distinction of having been shot and wounded by the commission surveyor, Andrew B. Gray, after an argument in which both men were apparently drunk. Subsequently, Weller became a senator from California, and he would use this office to loudly and successfully denounce Bartlett and the Whig administration on the Senate floor. In part as a result of Weller's agitation, the Senate Foreign Relations Committee, chaired by James M. Mason, a Democrat from Virginia, met in August 1852 to discuss the problems associated with the Mexican Boundary Survey. One of the committee's actions was to repudiate the compromise boundary line for southern and western New Mexico, a controversial plan that had been agreed to more than a year before by Bartlett and the Mexican commissioner. Two months later, Congress froze the appropriations for the Boundary Commission; the following March, Bartlett was removed as the U.S. Commissioner, in part on charges similar to those previously pressed against Weller. For an excellent discussion of the history of the survey of the U.S.-Mexican boundary, see Leon C. Metz, *Border* (El Paso: Mangan Books, 1989).

36. Senator Clarke's steadfast support of Bartlett would soon be repaid, at least in part, by Bartlett's appointment of Edward C. Clarke, the Senator's son, as assistant quartermaster on the Boundary Commission. During the winter of 1850–51, with the commission housed in what is now El Paso, Texas, plus the communities of San Elizario and Socorro a short distance downstream of El Paso along the Rio Grande, a fight broke out at a dance in Socorro, which by that time had become a haven for gamblers, drunkards, and prostitutes, as well as outcasts in general from the passing wagon trains. During the melee, young Clarke was

mortally stabbed and died the next day. A court was convened with a jury of six Americans and six Mexicans to try the ruffians suspected of the murder, and three men, all former employees on the commission, were found guilty and hanged. A fourth, and the principal suspect, was captured a short time later, brought to trial, found guilty, and also hanged. For a full account of this incident, see John Russell Bartlett, *Personal Narrative* (New York: D. Appleton & Company, 1854), vol. 1, pp. 157–166.

The Clarke killing was but one of many misfortunes that befell the Boundary Commission while under the direction of Bartlett. Prior to the Clarke incident, there were two other murders in the fall of 1850; these occurred when the Boundary Commission was on its march overland from the Texas coast to El Paso. In the summer of 1851, a Mexican teamster employed by the commission shot and killed an Apache at the Copper Mines of New Mexico. From October 12 to December 15, 1851, Bartlett was confined to quarters in Ures, Sonora, suffering from the effects of typhoid fever. On December 24, 1851, while still in Ures, Bartlett received word that his counterpart, Mexican Commissioner General Pedro García Conde, described by Bartlett as "a most amiable and estimable gentleman," had died five days before in his hometown of Arispe, Sonora, from the effects of a fever that had incapacitated him the previous three months. These incidents are also recorded in Bartlett's *Personal Narrative*, 1854, vol. 1.

After his recovery from typhoid fever, Bartlett rendezvoused with the main body of the commission at San Diego, California, on February 9, 1852. On his arrival there, he immediately got word that Thomas Harper, an assistant to Lieutenant A. W. Whipple on the survey of the Gila River, had drowned while swimming in the cold waters of the Colorado River. This tragedy occurred on December 19, 1851, at the river crossing near Fort Yuma. In his field journal for that date, Whipple writes,

> Poor Harper, an excellent and high minded man ever attentive to his duties ... and beloved by all who knew him has gone to swell

the list of victims to their insatiable river.... How little did I think that one of my own party would follow them to a watery grave in the same river" (*Whipple Journal*, Oklahoma State Historical Society).

An especially great personal loss for Bartlett was that of Lieutenant Colonel Louis S. Craig, head of Bartlett's military escort for nearly two years, who was murdered in the California desert on June 6, 1852, by two deserters from Fort Yuma. Of Col. Craig, Bartlett states, "His whole soul was absorbed in his profession.... His genuine kindness of heart, honesty of purpose, and rigid adherence to duty, had won for him a large circle of devoted friends among civilians, as well as among his brother officers" (*Personal Narrative*, 1854, vol. 2, pp. 146–147). According to Bartlett, Craig's body decomposed so quickly in the desert heat that the commissioner had no choice but to hold a simple funeral service and bury the colonel near their camp.

> The mortal remains of our excellent and much beloved friend, borne upon a cot by four soldiers, were consigned to his lonely grave. I read on the occasion the burial service of the Church of England.... In the silence that accompanied our sad and solitary rites, Wolfe's beautiful lines on the burial of Sir John Moore involuntarily suggested themselves to every mind (*Personal Narrative*, 1854, vol. 2, p. 145).

37. Bartlett and Fillmore maintained their relationship long after their service in the Federal government ceased. There is an original letter in the Rhode Island Historical Society Library from Fillmore to Bartlett, dated June 22, 1859, in which Fillmore thanks Bartlett for sending him a copy of the second edition of *Dictionary of Americanisms* (MSS 286–John Russell Bartlett Papers, Box 2, Folder 2, RIHS Library). In another letter from Fillmore to Bartlett, dated December 26, 1866, the former president thanks Bartlett for a set of books that were donated to the Buffalo Historical Society (Box 1, Folder 5, same source).

38. Bartlett was appointed Boundary Commissioner at a salary of $3,000.00 per year, a figure significantly higher than any salary he would later make as Rhode Island's Secretary of State. Bartlett's first choice as Commission Secretary, George Henry Moore, librarian of the New-York Historical Society, declined his offer, so Bartlett turned to his old friend from the 1820s and 1830s in Providence, Dr. Thomas H. Webb, who accepted the appointment at an annual salary of $1,500.00. After Bartlett and Webb returned to New England from the Southwest in 1853, and in anticipation of the passage of the Kansas-Nebraska Act in Congress, Thomas Webb became an organizer and officer of the Massachusetts Emigrant Aid Society, later to be merged into the New England Emigrant Aid Society. These, and similar societies in the Northeast, were organized to assist emigrants from the East to settle in Kansas, a scheme intended to insure that Kansas would eventually be admitted to the Union as a free state. Among the list of early abolitionist subscribers in Webb's venture was John Carter Brown of Providence, who purchased 50 shares at $20.00 each on March 14, 1855. Other Rhode Island subscribers include Moses B. Ives, Providence businessman and banker, who bought 25 shares on March 28, 1855, and businessman and future state governor, Seth Padelford, who bought 10 shares on May 7, 1855. For a full list of subscribers, see the *List of Subscriptions to Stock of the Massachusetts and New England Emigrant Aid Companies*, May 1854–June 1855, New England Emigrant Aid Company Collection, no. 624, Box 9, Folder 12, Kansas State Historical Society, 23 pages.

Among the other Bartlett appointees with ties to Rhode Island was George Thurber, a young chemist and pharmacist whose self-taught expertise in plants earned him the title of Commission Botanist, for which he was paid an annual salary of $800.00. Thurber and Webb were Bartlett's constant companions during their days together in the Southwest. Also during this period, Thurber sent occasional letters about commission activities back to Providence, and many of these accounts were published under his initials, G.T., in the *Providence Journal*. Years later, Thurber would become recognized as an authority on North American grasses; after serving on the faculty of what is now Michigan State University, he went on to serve as editor of the *American Agriculturist* for more than twenty years.

Two other young Rhode Islanders, Henry C. Cranston and Frank Wheaton, served on the Boundary Commission as chain bearers and station markers, each making a wage of $456.25 annually. Cranston, like Thurber, also published letters in the *Providence Journal* about commission activities, usually under his initials, H.C.C. There is a book of newspaper clippings related to commission activities in the Bartlett Papers at the John Carter Brown Library. All of the salary figures cited above are taken from *Senate Executive Document 119*, 1st Session, 32nd Congress, 1852, pp. 7–8.

39. Amiel Weeks Whipple (1817–1863), a lieutenant in the U.S. Corps of Topographical Engineers, had previously served on the Mexican Boundary Commission under Weller in California. He was retained by the commission under Bartlett and accomplished much in the field, including the survey of the proposed international boundary along the course of the Gila River, a line that ran from a point near Safford, Arizona, to the confluence of the Gila and Colorado rivers at Yuma. Whipple also set up astronomical observatories at many sites and helped determine the initial point on the Rio Grande for the Bartlett-Conde line for southern New Mexico, a compromise boundary that was later repudiated by Congress. In 1853–1854, Whipple led a government-sponsored expedition to search for a transcontinental railroad route from Fort Smith, Arkansas, to Los Angeles, California. While serving as a Union Army officer during the Civil War, Whipple was mortally wounded May 4, 1863, at the Battle of Chancellorsville. He was taken from the battlefield to Washington, D.C., where

he died a few days later, but not before President Lincoln promoted him to Brevet Major General. Fort Whipple (1863–1913) near Prescott, Arizona, was named in his honor.

40. Although published in two volumes of 1,130 total pages in 1854, *Personal Narrative* was also distributed in a limited edition of a single volume beginning in 1856. In 1965, Rio Grande Press reprinted the book in two volumes, adding a lengthy introduction by Odie B. Faulk. Volume 1 of the *Narrative* covers the period August 3, 1850, to February 9, 1852. It begins with the main body of the commission, comprised of 105 men and 260 tons of commission freight, leaving New York aboard the steamer, *Galveston*, bound for Indianola on the Texas coast. From Indianola, Bartlett describes the trip overland to San Antonio, and then on to El Paso, where by a previous agreement between the two governments, Bartlett was to meet his Mexican counterpart, General Pedro García Conde, in November 1850. After departing El Paso, Bartlett leads the reader to the Copper Mines (Santa Rita del Cobré) of New Mexico, where a large contingent of the commission headquartered from May 2, 1851, to August 27, 1851.

There were several incidents of note at the Copper Mines. First, encamped nearby was a large group of Apaches led by their notorious head chief, Mangas Colorado (Red Sleeve). Bartlett developed a good but vigilant relationship with the Apaches, providing them with gifts, food, etc., and on one occasion, he had the commission's tailor fashion a fine jacket for Mangas Colorado, who refused to wear the article in any manner other than tied around his waist. But there was another commodity in which the Indians manifested much interest. In a footnote to *Personal Narrative*, vol. 1, p. 302, Bartlett states, "In all my intercourse with the Indians, during the two and a half years I was in their country, I never gave one of them a drop of ardent spirits. I also prohibited others from doing so; but on a few occasions, had reason to suspect that my orders were disobeyed." On the same page, Bartlett writes about the repeated requests from the Apaches for whiskey.

They were constantly on the look-out for it, and when they saw a bottle they asked if it did not contain the coveted liquor. I one day handed them a bottle of catsup and another of vinegar, and told them to ascertain for themselves. A taste put a stop to their investigations, and they were afterwards less inquisitive.

Another incident involved Inez Gonzales, a young Mexican girl who had been stolen by Pinaleño Apaches from her relatives near Santa Cruz, Sonora, the previous September. On June 27, 1851, three traders from northern New Mexico stopped at Bartlett's camp to buy supplies, and in their possession was Inez Gonzalez, whom they had recently purchased from the Apaches, with the intent of taking her to Santa Fe. Bartlett exercised his authority under the Treaty of Guadalupe Hidalgo and had his military escort seize the girl. The following September 23, a small group from the commission traveled with Bartlett to Santa Cruz, where Bartlett personally returned Inez to her parents. According to Bartlett,

> I have witnessed many scenes on the stage, of the meeting of friends after a long separation ... but none of them approached in pathos the spontaneous burst of feeling exhibited by the mother and daughter on this occasion.... Although a joyful scene, it was a painfully affecting one to the spectators, not one of whom, could restrain his tears.... We then remounted our animals and proceeded towards the town in silence; and it was long before either party could compose themselves sufficiently to speak (*Personal Narrative*, vol. 1, pp. 402–403).

Two incidents occurred that led to confrontations and negotiations between Bartlett and Mangas Colorado. One involved two young Mexican boys, captives of the Apaches, who entered the tent of Bartlett's interpreter, John Cremony, and asked for protection from the Indians. Mangas Colorado and two of his sub-chiefs, Delgadito (Slender) and Ponce, confronted Bartlett and demanded the return of the boys, but the commissioner held firm in his determination to have the boys returned to their homes by the Mexican commissioner. Bartlett resolved the dispute when the chiefs accepted his offer of $250.00 worth of goods from the commissary store.

The other incident occurred when a Mexican teamster on the commission shot and killed one of the Apaches, the result being that Mangas Colorado and Ponce demanded that the killer be turned over to them for retribution. Bartlett insisted that the Mexican, now held prisoner by the commission, would be turned over to American authorities for prosecution. The Apaches finally agreed to this resolution of the case, and in return, Bartlett paid $30.00 from the Mexican's back wages to the mother of the dead Apache. The commissioner also agreed to make future payments to the mother at the teamster's customary wages of $20.00 per month.

Despite these difficulties, and the criticism Bartlett has received for befriending the Indians, it is important to note that the Apaches never brought bodily harm to Bartlett and his associates, even in cases where Bartlett and his colleagues were traveling in small parties through Apache-controlled country. Instead, the Apaches resorted more to stealing horses and mules from the commission and its military escort. The only direct attack from Indians occurred when Bartlett later traveled on the road between El Paso and Chihuahua City, and although Bartlett describes the attackers as Apaches, most authorities now believe the culprits were Comanches. This ambush resulted in two persons killed—one Mexican and one Indian.

Volume 2 of *Personal Narrative* covers the period February 11, 1852, in San Diego to late January 1853, when Bartlett returned to Providence. He spent the period February 24, 1852, to April 24, 1852, on a trip to San Francisco with a few officers of the commission, ostensibly to purchase new equipment and supplies for the commission's forthcoming overland trip from San Diego to El Paso. While Bartlett was in San Francisco, late winter rains brought floods to the major rivers east of San Francisco, and as a result, his plans for a trip to the California goldfields were cancelled. Instead, Bartlett and several of his colleagues rode on horseback the full length of Napa Valley and Knights Valley, then crossed over the Mayacmas Mountains and camped near, and explored among, the celebrated geysers along Big Sulphur Creek. See Jerry E. Mueller and Mark A. Walters, "Bartlett's Journey," *Bulletin*, Geothermal Resources Council, vol. 30, no. 6, 2001, pp. 238–242, for a more detailed description of Bartlett's trip to the geysers. Bartlett also visited the quicksilver mines at New Almaden south of San Francisco during this period. On the return trip to San Diego, Bartlett stopped for a few days at Monterey, which he predicted, "will become the residence of gentlemen of fortune. . . . It will be to San Francisco what Newport is now to New York" (*Personal Narrative*, vol. 2, p. 75). He also stopped at Los Angeles where he found that, "At the most miserable tavern in the back woods, I have found better accommodations than at this place" (*Personal Narrative*, vol. 2, p. 81). "Miserable" is a frequently used adjective in Bartlett's writing about his experiences in the Southwest!

In late May 1852, Bartlett and the bulk of his commission, now greatly reduced in number, left San Diego for Yuma on the Colorado River. From Yuma, the commission followed the Gila River upstream to the villages of the Maricopa Indians, a site that is south/southwest of present-day Phoenix. While following the course of the Gila, Bartlett stopped at two significant sites of Indian rock art, the best examples of which he transferred to his sketchbook. He would later incorporate these drawings into a series of plates for *Personal Narrative*. Leaving the Gila River, Bartlett traveled cross-country to Tucson, stopping en route to visit and sketch the Native American (Hohokam) ruins at Casa Grande, near what is now Coolidge, Arizona (see Fig. 26). From Tucson, Bartlett traveled south into northern Sonora, then eastward on both sides of what is now the international boundary, stopping briefly at Casas Grandes, Chihuahua, where he also took sketches and measurements of the ruins at Paquimé. Late in the evening of August 17, 1852, Bartlett and his advance party reached what is now El Paso, Texas, one day ahead of the rest of his fatigued party.

After leaving El Paso on October 8, 1852, Bartlett took a circuitous route through northeastern Mexico via Chihuahua City, Parras, Saltillo, and Monterey before reaching Ringgold Barracks on the lower Rio Grande on December 20, 1852. There, the commissioner met with his chief surveyor, Major W. H. Emory, who was running the boundary line downstream along the Rio Grande towards the Gulf of Mexico. At this point, and with word having been received from Washington on December 7, 1852, that the current year's appropriations for the Boundary Commission were frozen, Bartlett disbanded the field operations of the commission. He traveled to the Texas Coast and left Corpus Christi by boat on January 4, 1853, his commissionership all but over. He would never return to the West.

The oft-cited *Personal Narrative* remains an outstanding source on the conditions in the Southwest at the middle of the nineteenth century. Richly illustrated with oversize foldout maps and more than 100 woodcuts and lithographs, the book also contains 67 pages of supplementary commentary and appendices that Bartlett placed at the back of volume 2. *Personal Narrative* is, however, not without its faults. The book was obviously rushed into production, and as a result, there are numerous typographical errors, omissions, and redundancies that could have been avoided by careful editing. In volume 1, for example, the entry for August 31, 1851, on page 365, is followed by an entry for September 31 on page 367, although the next dated entry on page 368 is correctly listed as September 2. In volume 2, there is a lithograph of Tucson, Arizona, that appears following page 292, but the title of the illustration does not appear in the list of lithographs at the front of the volume. Also in volume 2, Bartlett lists woodcuts numbers 5 and 6 as California Indians, and he references them to page 34, but no such illustrations appear in the book. Bartlett's urgency to publish the book without thorough editing was likely prompted by many considerations, including the fact that he wanted to see his report on the boundary published before those of his successors and adversaries.

Personal Narrative was edited by William Wadden Turner, a noted linguist and philologist who, like Bartlett, had been active in the American Ethnological Society in New York City during the 1840s. By the time Bartlett wrote *Personal Narrative*, Turner had moved to Washington, D.C., to become Librarian of the U.S. Patent Office. In a letter to Bartlett dated November 8, 1853, Turner mentions he is having difficulty fitting the printer's five woodcuts of rock art (pictographs) into the space available in the text. However, Turner obviously succeeded, because the five woodcuts appear on pages 171–173 of volume 1 of the published book. Regrettably, Bartlett's original pencil field sketches of the rock art at Hueco Tanks, an area near El Paso, Texas, that is now a state historical park, are apparently lost. On November 27, 1853, Turner writes to inform Bartlett that nearly all of three edited chapters—to page 235 of volume 1—have been sent to D. Appleton and Company. Four days later, Turner writes again, this time to express his concern about Bartlett's decision to curtail the attractions of the book by limiting the number of illustrations. Turner is also wary about any attempts to speed up the editing process. On December 8, 1853, Turner writes to inform Bartlett that volume 1 is nearly complete; he also says he understands Bartlett's anxiety in wanting to get the book published. Unfortunately for Turner, he had agreed to wait for Bartlett to settle his Boundary Commission accounts with the government before requiring payment for his editorial services. As a consequence, Turner died in late 1859 without having been paid the $150.00 he was due, and his wife, through a representative, had to request payment from Bartlett in 1860 (see Turner to Bartlett,

April 12, 1859, and Randolph to Bartlett, September 22, 1860). The letters cited above are located in the Bartlett Papers at the John Carter Brown Library.

Personal Narrative is based largely on Bartlett's "Personal Journal," notes Bartlett recorded in a diary of his travels and exploits in the Southwest. It covers the period August 3, 1850, through December 6, 1852. The journal has never been fully transcribed and published, probably due to the fact that *Personal Narrative* contains almost all of the information that appears in the "Personal Journal," often verbatim, and the much larger book version is further enhanced by Bartlett's anecdotal information, the maps, and the illustrations. In addition, there are long passages in *Personal Narrative* that are a record of the exchanges between Bartlett and the Apache chiefs, transcriptions and translations made by Bartlett's interpreter, John Cremony, that do not appear in the "Journal."

There are, however, a few significant events in the "Journal" that do not appear in *Personal Narrative*. Under the entry for November 28, 1850, Bartlett writes about the latest dispatches he received in El Paso, including "letters from home announcing the death of my darling little Leila. I am overwhelmed with grief at the afflicting news and cannot realize it" (p. 69). On the following day, he adds,

> Passed a sleepless and painful night. My thoughts ... constantly on my distant home and family—of the loved ones I had left behind, and the deep affliction which the loss of my angel-child would cause to all. Felt quite ill, with headache, and distress in my stomach. Attributed it to the sudden shock I had had. Tried to rest during the day but could not. Mr. Thurber made me some ... tea in the evening after which I retired and soon got to sleep. ("Personal Journal," p. 70).

Another incident occurred in Santa Cruz, Sonora, two days after Bartlett had delivered Inez Gonzales to her parents. On September 25, 1851, Bartlett has a very long entry in his "Personal

Journal" that details a dispute and shouting match between Dr.
Thomas H. Webb, Commission Secretary, and Lieutenant Colonel J. D. Graham, Commission Principal Astronomer. Their dis-
agreement centered on the commission's lack of provisions and
the parties who were responsible for the shortage. The argument
further escalated into a discussion of who consumed the most
whiskey, Webb or Graham. Ultimately, Graham would challenge Webb to a duel, which Webb declined ("Personal Journal,"
pp. 169–171). Shortly thereafter, when calmer heads prevailed,
Graham left for the Copper Mines, and from there, he eventually
moved on to El Paso to head the boundary survey along the Rio
Grande. The disruptive Graham was soon replaced on the commission by W. H. Emory.

41. William H. Emory, *Report on the United States and Mexican Boundary Survey, Made Under the Direction of the Secretary of the Interior*
(Washington, D.C.: Government Printing Office, 1857–1859), 3
volumes.

   Although W. H. Emory, nicknamed "Bold Emory" during his
days at West Point, had worked on the Boundary Commission
under Weller in California, he was not an appointment to the
restructured commission under John Russell Bartlett. Instead,
Bartlett's commission began with the appointments of Andrew
B. Gray as Chief Surveyor and Lieutenant Colonel John McClellan as Principal Astronomer. Gray did not join Bartlett in the
field until July 19, 1851, by which time the commissioner had
moved his headquarters to the Copper Mines of New Mexico,
approximately 150 miles northwest of El Paso. Also by this time,
Bartlett and the Mexican Commissioner, confronted by errors
on the map appended to the Treaty of Guadalupe Hidalgo, had
agreed to a compromise boundary for southern and western New
Mexico. When Gray reached New Mexico and met with Bartlett,
he denounced the compromise as a violation of the intent of the
treaty.

   Early difficulties between Bartlett and McClellan led to the colonel's being recalled from the field at El Paso in late November 1850, before any of the survey on the boundary had commenced. McClellan was replaced by Lieutenant Colonel J. D. Graham, who did not arrive at El Paso until June 24, 1851, and Graham and Bartlett would not meet at the Copper Mines until August 2, 1851. Subsequent difficulties with Graham led to his being recalled from the field September 13, 1851, at a time when the colonel was in charge of the boundary survey along the Rio Grande. Assisting Graham at this time was Lieutenant Ambrose E. Burnside, Quartermaster and Commissary, who would later become one of Bartlett's closest associates in Rhode Island. With Graham's dismissal, Emory was appointed as Principal Astronomer, arriving in El Paso in November 1851 to lead the survey along the Rio Grande. Shortly thereafter, Gray was recalled as Chief Surveyor while in San Diego, and that position was also assigned to Emory. Thus we have a bizarre situation in which Emory, who had not yet met Bartlett in the field, was head of all of the scientific corps, and as he was working downstream along the Rio Grande in early 1852, the commissioner and a large section of the Boundary Commission were still in San Diego.

As an indication of how Emory viewed his position and how he perceived the role of Bartlett as a civilian commissioner, Emory wrote the following letter September 28, 1851, while en route to El Paso: "I am no asst. but in every way a co-equal of the Commissioner.... I have seen rather too much service to be an asst. to any man that has not a pair of epaulettes on his shoulder & who does not rank me in the Army," quoted in Robert V. Hine, *Bartlett's West* (New Haven: Yale University Press, 1968), p. 72. By the time Emory published his boundary report of 1857–1859, he and Bartlett had developed an acrimonious relationship, prompting Emory to include the following passages in his final report. Regarding the commission personnel he found upon reaching El Paso, Emory states,

with the exception of one or two, none were fitted for the service
on which they were engaged; most of them ignorant of the first
principles of surveying, and embroiled in feuds with each other,
and arrayed in hostility either to the commissioner or to the head
of the scientific corps (Emory, *Report*, vol. 1, p. 11).

In reference to the survey of the Rio Grande under his direction,
Emory writes,

> Superadded to the physical obstacles to be overcome, the men
> became almost insubordinate from the long absence of the com-
> missioner from the work, and his unpardonable neglect to furnish
> money for their payment. Some of them had not received any pay
> for eighteen months, and the commissioner was at the moment,
> with an equipage and corps of attendants, visiting the States of
> Chihuahua and Sonora, and the Geysers of California—places
> sufficiently distant from the line (Emory, *Report*, vol. 1, p. 12).

Emory goes on to challenge what he considered to be misrepre-
sentations of him by Bartlett.

> It is proper for me, however, before closing this chapter, to refer
> to a publication issued by Mr. J. R. Bartlett ... which professes
> to give an accurate account of the affairs of the commission. It is
> not my purpose to review that work, and expose its errors, but
> simply to correct some statements affecting myself.
>   Mr. Bartlett's principal achievement on the boundary was the
> agreement with General Conde, the Mexican commissioner, fix-
> ing the initial point on the Rio Bravo, in the parallel of 32° 22',
> instead of a point as laid down on the treaty map about eight
> miles above El Paso, which would have brought it to the par-
> allel of 31° 52'. That agreement is no less remarkable than the
> adroitness and success with which Mr. Bartlett convinced the
> authorities at Washington of its correctness.... Mr. Bartlett, in
> his account of the matter, states I was ordered to sign the map of
> his initial point, and that I did sign it. But he does not state what
> was the purport or meaning of my signature....
>   I refused to recognize the act as that of the joint commission,

and I signed the map as the order directed, carefully and studiously attaching a certificate that it was the initial point of the two commissioners ... and nothing else (Emory, *Report*, vol. 1, pp. 16–17).

Emory was also irritated by the fact that Bartlett chose in his *Personal Narrative* (vol. 2, p. 212) to suggest Emory's earlier map of the Gila River grossly underrepresents the true size of the curves in the river near Gila Bend. According to Emory,

> It would have been no more than truth required, for Mr. Bartlett to have stated, what I expressly state in my printed memoir accompanying this map, that I did not explore this bend, but laid it down from conjecture. It is a small affair, subtended by a chord of thirty or forty miles (Emory, *Report*, vol. 2, p. 17).

The historian William Goetzmann describes Emory's final boundary report as follows:

> In organization and style of writing, Emory's *Report* was much inferior to that of his rival, Frémont. Following the Humboldt example, Emory conceived of his subject in chapters which were topical essays, thus including much that was repetitious. His own narrative of the boundary operations was brief and confined to an unsystematic account of his labors and an inappropriate castigation of the behavior of Commissioner Bartlett (pp. 16–18).... The result of this method of organization produced no really clear picture of the operation of the survey itself. Such a picture remains buried among the archives of the Commission. The scientific content of the Report, however, was of the greatest significance, and it equaled the findings of Frémont (William H. Goetzmann, *Army Exploration of the American West, 1803–1863* [New Haven: Yale University Press, 1959], pp. 198–199).

Goetzmann goes on to describe Bartlett's *Personal Narrative*:

> Bartlett's book ranks alongside those of Frémont, Parkman, and Gregg as a classic. Within its pages is contained a panoramic view of the way of life of an entire region previously known only to a few. It was to be of little use to scientists, but for many a hammock

reader at Saratoga or Newport it opened up an exciting America and helped create an image of the exotic West (Goetzmann, 1959, p. 206).

42. James Gadsden (1788–1858) was not a general from Texas, and he did not succeed Bartlett as Boundary Commissioner. Gadsden, the Minister to Mexico under Franklin Pierce, negotiated the Gadsden Treaty of 1854, under which Mexico ceded portions of southern Arizona and southern New Mexico to the United States for ten million dollars. The Gadsden Purchase resolved the last of the remaining boundary issues between the two countries; it also rendered the compromise boundary previously agreed to by Bartlett and his Mexican counterpart, General Pedro García Conde, null and void. Bartlett was replaced as Boundary Commissioner in 1853 by Robert B. Campbell who, like Gadsden, was from South Carolina. After the Gadsden Treaty was ratified in 1854, Major William H. Emory was appointed commissioner to run the survey of the land boundary from El Paso, Texas, to Yuma, Arizona.

43. Henry Bowen Anthony (1815–1884) was a graduate of Brown University, an editor and publisher of the *Providence Journal*, a two-term governor of Rhode Island, and a U.S. Senator from the state from 1859 to 1884. According to the *Providence Directory*, Anthony lived at 5 Benevolent Street, just east of Benefit Street, and a short distance from the Providence Athenaeum. Surprisingly, Bartlett's name is not listed at the Anthony address in the directories for 1854 or 1855–56. However, in the directory of 1857, John R. Bartlett is listed at the Benevolent Street address, and Henry A. Bartlett, presumably his son, is listed as a clerk at 6 South Water Street in Providence, although the latter boarded at 21 College Street. The residences of the two Bartletts remain the same in the directory of 1858, but for 1859, there is no listing for Henry A. Bartlett. In the directory of 1861, John Russell Bartlett is still at the Henry B. Anthony address, and Henry A. Bartlett reappears at 149 Benefit Street. By 1862, Anthony's address

remains the same; Henry A. Bartlett is no longer listed because he was in the Civil War; and John Russell Bartlett has moved to 147 Benefit Street. Thus it appears John Russell Bartlett lived with Henry B. Anthony for at least five years. The Anthony House, a 2.5 story Greek Revival structure built in 1844, still stands at 5 Benevolent Street and is now owned by Brown University.

Widely known for his literary pursuits, in 1882 Henry B. Anthony acquired a collection of 6,000 volumes of poetry that had been started by Albert Gorton Greene (1802–1868), a noted Providence lawyer and poet. After Greene's death, the bulk of the poetry collection was purchased by Caleb Fiske Harris (1818–1881), a prominent businessman and book collector, who added many volumes of poetry to the collection, as well as songs, ballads, and plays. Following the death of Harris and his wife in a canoeing accident in Maine in 1881, the collection of American poetry was held for a brief time by a Providence publisher and bookseller, Sidney S. Rider, who sold the collection in 1882 to Anthony, a cousin to Caleb Fiske Harris. Anthony died two years later, bequeathing his collection to the Brown University Library, with the stipulation that this special collection would remain intact and be designated the "Harris Collection of American Poetry." Subsequently, this famous collection received a substantial endowment from Albert Gorton Greene's son-in-law, Samuel Coffman Eastman (1837–1917). There are now more than 250,000 items in the Harris Collection of American Poetry and Plays. See Mark N. Brown et al., Leslie T. Wendel, ed., *Special Collections at Brown University: A History and Guide* (Providence: The Friends of the Library of Brown University, 1988).

There can be little doubt that the Bartlett family held Henry B. Anthony in high regard. Bartlett's son, Henry Anthony Bartlett, and Bartlett's grandson, Henry Anthony Duvillard, were named after Henry B. Anthony. Also, Ida Russell Bartlett Mowry, Bartlett's granddaughter and the daughter of John Russell Bartlett, Jr., bequeathed a portrait of Henry B. Anthony to the Rhode Island Historical Society in 1964. According to Ida Mowry's daughter, Margaret Gummere, that portrait of Henry Anthony was for many years prominently displayed on a wall in the Mowry home, alongside a portrait of John Russell Bartlett. Because the two men had been painted late in life when both had long, flowing beards, the Mowry family affectionately referred to the two men in the portraits as "the Smith Brothers," referring to the icon of a popular patented cough medicine. For a brief biography of Anthony, see *Henry Bowen Anthony: A Memorial*, by the Rhode Island General Assembly (Providence: E. L. Freeman & Company, 1885).

44. During the 1850s, when John Russell Bartlett, Jr., was living with the Jacobs family in Massachusetts, Henry Anthony Bartlett apparently was living with his grandfather, Smith Bartlett, at Cape Vincent, New York. There are letters in the Bartlett papers at the John Carter Brown Library in which Henry writes to his father in Providence to complain about the high costs being charged by his grandfather for Henry's upkeep, especially for firewood. As we shall see, both of Bartlett's sons would go on to have distinguished careers of their own.

At the start of the Civil War, Henry Bartlett left with the 1st Rhode Island Regiment of Volunteers and saw action in the First Battle of Bull Run. Shortly thereafter, he was appointed an officer in the Marine Corps, retiring from that service with the rank of major in 1898. Henry had the distinction of having been shipwrecked and rescued twice during his military career, including once in the Indian Ocean where he and several comrades survived forty hours on a raft before being saved by a passing ship. Henry, as well as John, Jr., participated in the survey of a proposed canal route across the Isthmus of Tehuantepec in southern Mexico. Later in his career, Henry was stationed in Washington, D.C., where he held the title of Judge Advocate of the Marine Corps. Originally married to Edith Blankman of New York, who died in 1877, Henry later married Cara Hall, daughter of Oakley Hall, the former mayor of New York City. Henry, who resided in New York City during his few years of retirement, died in Atlantic City, New Jersey in 1901 (see Fig. 13).

John Russell Bartlett, Jr., entered the U.S. Naval Academy in 1859 at age 16, and subsequently distinguished himself during a long naval career, retiring initially in 1897 with the rank of captain. He reentered the service as a volunteer when the war with Spain broke out in 1898, assuming the dual roles of Chief of Naval Intelligence and Superintendent of the Coast Signal Service. John, Jr., retired again from the Navy in late 1898 and spent the rest of his life with his wife, Jeanie R. Jenckes, at the Jenckes family homestead in Lonsdale, just north of Providence, Rhode Island. By an act of Congress in 1903, and in recognition of his devoted service to the country, John, Jr., was promoted to Rear Admiral on the list of retired officers.

Like his father, John, Jr., also wrote articles and delivered papers before learned societies. For example, he read a paper entitled "Deep-Sea Soundings and Temperatures in the Gulf Stream" at the American Association for the Advancement of Science meeting in Montreal in 1882. One of John Russell Bartlett, Jr.'s, greatest honors came in 1898 when Brown University awarded him an Honorary Doctorate of Science. At the time of his death in 1904, John, Jr., was on the Board of Directors of the *Providence Journal* (see Fig. 14).

Information on John Russell Bartlett, Jr., comes from the *Russell Family Genealogy* (1879) and a series of newspaper articles held in the Archives of Brown University, including the *Providence Evening Telegram* (undated); the *Providence Bulletin* (November 23, 1904); and the *Providence Journal* (July 10, 1898, and March 7, 1902). The information on Henry Anthony Bartlett is taken from the *Russell Family Genealogy* (1879) and, "In Memoriam: Henry Anthony Bartlett, Major, U.S. Marine Corps, retired," a *Military Order of the Loyal Legion of the United States*, San Francisco, September 13, 1901.

45. In reviewing the records of state election results for the years 1855–1871, it is apparent that Bartlett was indeed a popular Secretary of State. For the entire seventeen-year period, he received 79.5 percent of the votes, although that figure is skewed by the fact he ran unopposed for six consecutive years from 1860 to 1865. When those six years are excluded from the analysis, Bartlett received, on average, 66.4 percent of the total votes cast; the rest of the votes were won by designated opposition candidates and write-ins. Given that Bartlett's plurality in the state elections was very strong throughout the period he served, it is understandable why he expressed astonishment at his not being renominated for the office in 1872.

Bartlett's exuberance about the one time he received every vote is somewhat tempered because that result occurred in an election year in which he ran unopposed—1860. Bartlett further indicates that Seth Padelford and William Sprague were also candidates that year, but he neglects to mention that those two gentlemen were the principal candidates for governor, not Secretary of State. What Bartlett should have stated is that he got all of the 23,341 votes cast for Secretary of State in 1860, and although he ran unopposed, there were also no write-in votes against him. Thus, as the election committee for 1860 noted in its final report, Bartlett was elected unanimously, the only time he accomplished that feat. This information is taken from a series of annual election reports on file with the State Archives Division of the Office of Secretary of State, Providence, Rhode Island.

46. At the time Bartlett was compiling his *Bibliography of Rhode Island*, Elisha Reynolds Potter (1811–1882) was a member of the Rhode Island Senate, having previously served as a state and federal representative. From 1868 to 1882, Potter was a justice on the Rhode Island Supreme Court.

47. In a letter to Bartlett dated August 3, 1863, Billings indicates the two paintings will be shipped via steamer from London on August 5, 1863 (Bartlett Papers, John Carter Brown Library).

48. Emanuel Gottlieb Leutze (1816–1868) was a noted German-American painter of portraits and, especially, historical events. He is perhaps best known for his 1851 portrayal of *Washington Crossing the Delaware*, a painting of gigantic dimensions that is owned by the Metropolitan Museum of Art. Equally large is his mural commissioned for the U.S. Capitol, *Westward the Course of Empire Takes its Way*, a depiction of American frontier settlement. For a fuller account of Leutze and a catalog of his works, see Barbara S. Groseclose, *Emanuel Leutze, 1816–1868: Freedom Is the Only King* (Washington, D.C.: Smithsonian Institution Press, 1975). Interestingly, this volume lists only one known Leutze painting of Burnside, a 30 × 24" portrait that was found in Leutze's studio when the artist died in 1868; there is no mention of the much larger Burnside portrait commissioned by Bartlett.

Ambrose Everett Burnside (1824–1881) was a West Point graduate and a Brigadier General and Major General during the Civil War, fighting and commanding with mixed success in numerous battles including First Bull Run, Antietam, Fredericksburg, The Wilderness, Spotsylvania, and Petersburg. After the Civil War, Burnside was a three-term Governor of Rhode Island, and from 1875 to 1881 he was a U.S. Senator from the state. The painting of Burnside commissioned from Leutze by Bartlett was paid for by subscriptions totaling $1,675.00. Listed among the individuals and companies contributing $100.00 each are John Carter Brown, A & W Sprague, and the Burnside Rifle Company. Among the $50.00 contributors is Thomas A. Jenckes, a prominent lawyer in New York and Providence and the future father-in-law of John Russell Bartlett, Jr.

The canvas of the Leutze painting of Burnside, painted from life, measures 113" high by 73" wide, and is signed and dated 1863. It is a full length, oblique view of the general in military uniform. One hand of Burnside rests on his sword; the other rests on a hip and holds field glasses. As Burnside looks into the distance, his hat rests at his feet, inclined across the top of a series of rolled battlefield maps. In a letter to Bartlett dated February 26, 1863, Leutze writes, "The background and accessories we selected are from ... Antietem, and I am sure I can make a striking picture of it." In subsequent letters to Bartlett, Leutze indicates the painting was shipped to Bartlett in late April 1863, and payment in full was received on May 9, 1863. For a biography of Burnside, see Benjamin Perley Poore, *The Life and Public Services of Ambrose E. Burnside: Soldier—Citizen—Statesman, with an Introduction by Henry B. Anthony* (Providence: J. A. & R. A. Reid, 1882).

49. The following information is taken from Reuben Aldridge Guild, *History of Brown University, with Illustrative Documents* (Providence: Providence Press Company, 1867). In the introduction to his chapter on the "Collection of Portraits," Guild writes: "Most of them have been obtained, it will be observed, through the active exertions of the Hon. John R. Bartlett, to whom the thanks of a grateful public are justly due." Of the following list of the thirty-one original portraits, Guild attributes numbers 6–19 and numbers 21–26 to the efforts of Bartlett. Although Bartlett leaves blank the year in which he began to collect the portraits, it is likely he started in 1856, or possibly early 1857 at the latest. The evidence for this assumption is found in a series of letters written by the artist Henry C. Pratt of Boston. On April 14, 1857, Pratt reminds Bartlett that someone needs to decide which portrait of the Rev. William Ellery Channing is to be copied by Pratt (see item 19 below). Pratt writes again to Bartlett on July 7, 1857, and asks if a decision has been made on the Channing painting because the artist is eager to begin work. On August 26, 1857, Pratt informs Bartlett that the head of Rev. George Berkeley is nearly complete; then Pratt asks if any accessories such as books should be added to the portrait (see item 18 below). The following month, on September 23, 1857, Pratt notifies Bartlett that the two portraits are ready to be shipped at a cost of $125.00 each. At the end of September 1857, Pratt informs Bartlett that the artist has received a draft of $125.00, an amount equal to the cost of

one painting. These letters are in the Bartlett Papers at the John Carter Brown Library, along with a note written by Bartlett in 1857 that indicates he paid Henry Pratt $135.00 for two paintings and another $2.00 for "boxing the same" (Bartlett Papers, Box 13, *Miscellaneous Papers*, John Carter Brown Library). Presumably, the receipt is for the cost of the second painting, not both paintings as stated by Bartlett. Another possibility is that the receipt is in reference to some paintings Bartlett bought from Pratt for his private collection.

Each entry below contains the name of the subject; the name of the artist; the Brown University portrait number; and the current location of the painting. This information is taken from Robert P. Emlen, "Lists of the Brown Portrait Collection," a compilation originally submitted to the Brown University Library on August 20, 1997, and updated in January 1999.

1. Rev. James Manning, D.D., painted by Cosmo Alexander, BP1, University Hall.

2. Rev. James Manning, D.D., copy by James Sullivan Lincoln, BP3, Sayles Hall.

3. Nicholas Brown, painted by Chester Harding, BP2, Sayles Hall.

4. Rev. Francis Wayland, D.D., LL.D., painted by George P. A. Healy, BP4, Sayles Hall.

5. Rev. Adoniram Judson, D.D., painted by George P. A. Healy, BP5, unlocated.

6. William Coddington, copy by Thomas Mathewson, BP6, John Hay Library.

7. Esek Hopkins, painted by M. J. Heade, no current information.

8. Abraham Whipple, copy by M. J. Heade, BP167, John Hay Library.

9. Moses Brown, painted by M. J. Heade, BP7, sold.

10. Colonel William Barton, copy by James Sullivan Lincoln, BP8, John Hay Library.

11. Gilbert Stuart, painted by Jane Stuart, BP9, sold.

12. Samuel Slater, painted by James Sullivan Lincoln, BP10, sold in 1980.

13. Thomas Poynton Ives, copied by James Sullivan Lincoln, BP11, John Hay Library.

14. Tristam Burges, LL.D., painted by C. B. King, BP12, Sayles Hall.

15. Henry Wheaton, LL.D., copy by M. J. Heade, BP13, John Hay Library.

16. Commodore Oliver Perry, copy by Jane Stuart, BP14, sold in 1980.

17. Asher Robbins, LL.D., Painted by Charles King, BP15, sold in 1980.

18. Rev. George Berkeley, D.D., copy by Henry C. Pratt, BP16, sold.

19. Rev. William Ellery Channing, D.D., copy by Henry C. Pratt, BP17, John Hay Library.

20. Rev. Nathan B. Crocker, D.D., painted by D. Huntington, BP18, John Hay Library storage.

21. Major-General Ambrose E. Burnside, painted by Emanuel Leutze, BP189, on loan to the Rhode Island State House.

22. Brigadier-General Isaac P. Rodman, painted by James Sullivan Lincoln, BP19, John Hay Library.

23. Lt. Colonel Christopher Greene, copy by James Sullivan Lincoln, BP20, John Hay Library.

24. Dr. Solomon Drowne, copy by C. C. Ingham, BP21, John Hay Library.

25. Charles II, King of England, attributed to John B. Gaspars, BP22, John Hay Library.

26. Catherine of Braganza, Queen of England, attributed to John B. Gaspars, BP23, John Hay Library.

27. Rev. William Rogers, copy by Eliza J. Rogers, BP24, University Hall.

28. Dr. Levi Wheaton, painted by George P. A. Healy, BP25, John Hay Library.

29. Gen. James Talmadge, LL.D., engraving by unknown artist, no current information.

30. Oliver Cromwell, painted by M. J. Heade, BP26, sold in 1980.

31. General Andrew Jackson, painted by Jacques G. L. Amans, BP27, sold in 1980.

50. Henry Whitney Bellows (1814–1882) was minister of the First Congregational (Unitarian) Church in New York City, and at the time of Bartlett's second marriage to Ellen Eddy, Bellows was also president of the United States Sanitary Commission—a precursor to the American Red Cross—which served the needs of soldiers during and after the Civil War. Bartlett received a silver tray as a wedding present from John Carter Brown, for whom Bartlett had been personal librarian for nearly a decade. That tray, now owned by the John Carter Brown Library, carries the following inscription:

John Russell Bartlett / From / John Carter Brown /
November 10, 1863

The following unsigned and undated poem, apparently written by Ellen Eddy, was saved by Bartlett (Box 13 of his Miscellaneous Papers at the John Carter Brown Library):

Dear Mr. B—Good Mr. B—
Do for a while attend to me.
Nothing but in old records musing
Or with assemblymen carousing
Will soon convert you to a very
Ancient, brass mounted secretary.
Then close your books as you are told
And praise my locks of shining gold.
And say my eyes are bright & fine
And be a darling valentine.

Ellen Eddy Bartlett, born March 10, 1829, was 34 years old when she married John Russell Bartlett, who was then age 58. She died September 6, 1913, having outlived her husband by twenty-seven years. Ellen is buried in the Swan Point Cemetery in Providence, not with John Russell Bartlett in the Bartlett family plot, but instead is interred a short distance away with her parents in the Eddy family plot. Her grave is marked with a very small stone on which the raised initials E. E. B. appear on the curved top of the granite. Details of her birth and death, and her marriage to John Russell Bartlett, are carved on the side of the Eddy family monument. According to the *Providence Directory*, Ellen Bartlett occupied the house at 225 Benefit Street until her death in 1913.

51. According to the U. S. Census of 1880, the Bartlett household at 225 Benefit Street consisted of the following:

John R. Bartlett, head of house and retired Rhode Island Secretary of State, age 74.

Ellen E. Bartlett, housewife, born in 1833, age 47. The year of her birth must be an error in the census because all other records show her year of birth to be 1829.

Henry A. Bartlett, Captain, U. S. Navy, age 41, widower. Henry was a career officer in the marines and probably used his father's residence in Providence as his permanent address.

Anna R. Duvillard, no occupation, age 44, widow. Bartlett's oldest surviving daughter apparently returned to Providence to live with her father after her husband died in New York.

Henry A. Duvillard, son of Anna and Bartlett's grandson, age 20, mechanical engineer. Henry spent the rest of his life in Providence, working for a time as an engineer at the Corliss Steam Engine Company. For approximately fifty years, he lived at 173 George Street, a short distance from Brown University.

Ann Cashon, age 40, and Jane Pollard, age 28, servants.

52. Bartlett's elaborate scrapbooks on subjects relating to the history of the Civil War, more than fifty volumes, are housed in the Special Collections of the Providence Public Library. Each volume has the following typeset and printed title page: "History of the Great Conspiracy and Rebellion in the United States Gleaned from the Newspapers of the Day, Embracing a Daily Record of Events, Narratives, Letters, Military and Naval Orders, Official Reports and Documents, Speeches, Lectures, Statistics, Editorial Comments, etc., Commencing in September 1860." In addition, Bartlett produced scrapbooks on other topics relating to the Civil War, including two thick volumes on the "Ballads of the Rebellion." The latter two scrapbooks—the gift of Bartlett's heirs in 1915—are held by the Providence Athenaeum.

The Athenaeum also holds several other scrapbooks by Bartlett. The smallest and simplest of these is a volume called, "The Japanese Embassy to the U.S." Much more impressive is a single, thick volume of clippings, maps, diagrams, etc., entitled, "The Atlantic Telegraph: Its Origin and History. With an account of the voyages of the steamers Niagara and Agamemnon in laying the cable; and of the celebration of the great event, in New York, Philadelphia, Brooklyn, Montreal, Dublin, Paris, etc. . . . arranged by John Russell Bartlett. 1858." Equally impressive is a two-volume set on "The Assassination of James A. Garfield, President of the United States." This work is divided into three sections: section one covers the period from when Garfield was wounded to when he died (September 19, 1881); section two deals with the ceremonies held in Washington and Cleveland at the time of Garfield's funeral; and the last section is an account of the trial, conviction, and execution of Garfield's assassin. According to the printed title page, the Garfield volumes were "Collected and arranged by John Russell Bartlett. Providence, 1881–1882."

More recently, an untitled scrapbook by Bartlett, this one dealing with Abraham Lincoln, has come to light. It consists of a long address on Lincoln that was given before Congress on February 12, 1866, by the noted historian George Bancroft. Bartlett extra-illustrated the printed address, then added much Lincoln memorabilia at the end of the volume. Included in the Lincoln scrapbook are copies of letters that were exchanged between Bartlett and Mary Lincoln in late 1865 and early 1866. There is also a copy of a letter that Senator Henry B. Anthony, Bartlett's brother-in-law, wrote to Mary Lincoln, supporting Bartlett's request to Mrs. Lincoln for materials to be used in a book about her late husband. According to Philip A. Metzger of the Lehigh University Library, the scrapbook is one of approximately 800 Civil War-era items that Lehigh acquired from Bartlett in 1885, less than a year before Bartlett's death.

53. Although Bartlett is widely known for his assistance to the Brown family in the development of their great private library, the Bibliotheca Americana, little has thus far been published about Bartlett's own library, a major collection that apparently was divided among family members after his death in 1886. Fortunately, Bartlett's library, housed at his residence at 225 Benefit Street, was still intact when visited by Horatio Rogers in the late 1870s. Thereafter, Rogers wrote a book, *Private Libraries of Providence* (Providence: Sidney S. Rider, 1878), in which he devotes a full chapter (pp. 135–146) to the Bartlett collection.

Based on Rogers's comments, it appears Bartlett's holdings were concentrated in the areas of geography, ethnology, antiquities, philology, history, and the classics. According to Rogers (pp. 135–136):

> A glance along his shelves reveals the lines of research he delights to follow, and at once opens up to the observer the literary character of the man. His is essentially a working library. To understand, however, that, by the use of this term, is implied a lack of choice editions or of fine bindings, would be a gross misapprehension. By it is meant, simply, that the books of this collection are, to a large extent, his tools, so to speak, and not merely the recreation of his leisure hours.

Rogers notes the large collection of Civil War books and the associated scrapbooks Bartlett prepared on the subject. He also mentions the books in the library that were written by Bartlett himself, along with the many volumes that Bartlett extra-illustrated. However, the real strengths of the library lay in the books, some quite rare, dealing with the following subjects: accounts of voyages and explorations for a Northwest passage; antiquities of the Mideast, southern Europe, and the British Isles; the latest works on prehistoric man, especially those by British authors; a large number of dictionaries, including John Baret's *Alvearie*, compiled in English, French, Greek and Latin and printed in London in 1580; a number of works on Homer, of which Rogers indicates Bartlett had a copy of F. J. Du Roveray's edition (probably 1813) of Alexander Pope's translation of the *Iliad* and the *Odyssey*, in twelve octavo volumes; many sets of journals and transactions of learned societies; and six missals probably produced before A.D. 1400. Rogers further states (p. 145) that "The number of presentation copies ... with the autograph or book-plate of the author, or of other distinguished men, is quite remarkable."

54. Bartlett uses the term "sketch" to describe his short essays or descriptions of the individual officers covered in his book; he is not referring to the illustrations of the officers as sketches. The

engraved portraits in his book are actually engraved black and white photographs.

55. Unfortunately, Bartlett never prepared a complete list of his publications. Missing in his autobiography are citations to nearly all of his articles published in newspapers, magazines, journals, and encyclopedias. Among the more important outlets for Bartlett's lesser-known works are: *American Anthropologist*; *American Cyclopaedia*; *American Whig Review*; *The Bookmart*; *Historical Magazine*; *Literary World*; and the *Magazine of American History*. There is a second compilation of Bartlett's publications, written in his hand in approximately 1880, among the Bartlett Papers at the John Carter Brown Library. This second effort provides little useful additional information.

56. *Progress of Ethnology* was printed by William Van Norden, to whom Bartlett paid $33.00 on May 3, 1847, for 250 copies of the book. (Bartlett Papers, Box 13, Miscellaneous Papers, John Carter Brown Library).

57. This book is largely a compilation of previously existing material that was collected, organized, and presented in published form by Bartlett. As part of the events leading up to the celebration of the country's centennial, Bartlett also published a major article on the *Gaspee* incident in the *Providence Daily Journal*, June 10, 1875.

58. Copies of this work were presented by Bartlett as gifts to a number of prominent citizens, including Henry B. Anthony, John Carter Brown, William Gammell, Desmond FitzGerald, Caleb Fiske Harris, and Thomas A. Jenckes. Also, the published book states that 60 copies were printed in 4to, rather than the 80 copies Bartlett cites in his memoirs.

59. At the time Bartlett wrote this section of his memoirs in 1867, his printed catalogues of the Bibliotheca Americana, though significant, paled in comparison to the magnificent volumes he would produce for John Carter Brown and the Brown family between 1870 and 1882. Thus, it is surprising that he would not

have updated this section of his memoirs. The following is a complete chronology of Bartlett's printed work on the catalogues of the Bibliotheca Americana:

1865. Part I. 1493–1600. 79 pages. 302 entries.

1866. Part II. 1601–1700. 249 pages. 1,160 entries. Index to Parts I & II.

1870. Part III. 1701–1771. Volume I. 446 pages. 1,809 entries.

1871. Part III. 1772–1800. Volume II. 554 pages. 2,364 entries. Index to all of Part III.

1875. Part I. 1482–1600. 526 pages. 600 entries. 121 figures. Index. Revised 1865 volume.

1882. Part II. 1601–1700. 647 pages. 1,642 entries. 113 figures. Index. Revised 1866 volume.

60. The treatment of individual officers in this volume appears to be largely the result of public information that was readily available to Bartlett, plus whatever additional material he was able to solicit from the officers and their families. Thus, the coverage of individual officers is quite uneven. For example, Bartlett devotes eighty-five pages to just one officer—General Ambrose E. Burnside. In a letter to Bartlett dated January 4, 1866, Burnside is obviously pleased with the engraved photo of himself that Bartlett had obtained for the book (MSS 286–John Russell Bartlett Papers, Box 1, Folder 5, Rhode Island Historical Society Library).

Another officer in this volume is Brevet General Major Frank Wheaton, a native of Providence who fought in many major battles ranging from Bull Run to Petersburg. Earlier, Bartlett had appointed Wheaton to the Mexican Boundary Commission when Wheaton was only seventeen years old, and he proved to be an invaluable assistant to Lieutenant A. W. Whipple on the commission's survey of the Gila River in Arizona. Whipple, in an

entry to his field journal dated October 27, 1851, credits Wheaton with having made a pencil sketch of a deep canyon along the
Gila River, a spectacular scene that was subsequently redrawn in
pencil by Bartlett and watercolored by Seth Eastman. Bartlett's
pencil sketch of this scene, *Great Canyon of the Gila*, is drawing
number 173a in the Bartlett Collection at the John Carter Brown
Library, and Seth Eastman's watercolor version, *Great Cañon, Rio
Gila*, is catalogued as number 47.112.9 at the Rhode Island School
of Design. The field site of Wheaton's drawing was rediscovered in a remote area of eastern Arizona in October 2003. It was
found at the eastern (upstream) end of the Needles Eye by a small
exploration party consisting of Harry Hewitt, Tom Jonas, and
myself, with David Miller as our trip organizer and leader. Other
than some encroachment by vegetation along the floor of the canyon, especially salt-cedar (tamarisk), the scene today is virtually
identical to that sketched by Wheaton in 1851.

61. The published title of this paper is *Pre-historic Man and His Associates*, not *Primeval Man and His Associates* as listed by Bartlett for
the title of his presentations. Bartlett's paper appeared a mere
nine years after the publication of Charles Darwin's *Origin of Spe-
cies*, which ignited a debate about evolution in general and the
evolution of man in particular. At the same time, geologists such
as Sir Charles Lyell were looking at the sedimentary record to
try to determine the age of the Earth, and among geographers
the concept of "environmental determinism" was emerging to
explain the impact and control of the environment, especially climate, on man and his activities. Walking a tightrope among all
these ideas, Bartlett offered the following balanced statement on
page 31 of his paper: "Thoughtful and well informed men are now
prepared to believe that the earth has existed for untold ages, and
·that man may have dwelt upon it ever since it became adapted
to his wants."

62. The Wantons produced four colonial governors of Rhode Island:
William 1732–1733; John 1734–1740; Gideon 1745–1746 and 1747–

1748; and, Joseph 1769–1775. Bartlett published a shorter account of the Wanton Family in the *Providence Journal* in 1871.

63. This work was actually published in 1870 as a serial of 71 pages total in *Historical Magazine*. It represented an update of a series of articles on the same subject published by Bartlett in the *Providence Journal* in 1860–1861.

64. The Sopori Land and Mining Company at one time controlled 31 square leagues, or approximately 250 square miles, of desert terrain south of Tucson, Arizona. The property extended from near the Mission of San Xavier del Bac on the north to the Presidio of Tubac on the south, and from the Santa Rita Mountains on the east to the Baboquivari Mountains on the west. The tract was traversed from south to north by the small but perennial Santa Cruz River. When the Sopori Company incorporated in Rhode Island in 1859, at a time when Bartlett was Secretary of State, John Russell Bartlett was listed as secretary of the company and a member of the corporation's board of directors. Nearly all of the members of the board were from Rhode Island, including Bartlett's brother-in-law, Henry B. Anthony. Among the few outsiders was Samuel Colt of the Colt Firearms Company, Hartford, Connecticut. Another exception was Sylvester Mowry, who at that time was from Arizona. As a prelude to the establishment of the company, the *Providence Daily Journal* ran a front-page exchange on March 3, 1858, between Mowry and Bartlett that describes the opportunities for settlement in Arizona, including the potential for agricultural and mining development. Little is known of the Sopori Company's success, but in a letter to Bartlett dated May 27, 1881, Frederic M. Sackett describes how he bought all 4,438 shares of the company after it defaulted on an assessment (Bartlett Papers, John Carter Brown Library).

Sylvester Mowry was born in Providence January 17, 1833, and graduated from West Point in 1852. After a few years in the Army in the West, he resigned his commission to become a land and mining promoter in what is now southern Arizona, even serving at one time as an unofficial delegate to Congress from the Arizona Territory. During the Civil War, Mowry was arrested at his silver mines in the Patagonia Mountains some fifty-five miles south/southeast of Tucson and jailed for several months in the territorial prison at Yuma for aiding the Confederates, a charge for which he was never convicted. Mowry became ill in approximately 1870, sought treatment in England, and died there in 1871.

Still highly regarded in Arizona for his early-day promotion and development of the state, Mowry is, by contrast, regarded mostly as a charlatan in New Mexico. There, his name was given to a land development scheme along the Mimbres River, the site of a small village promoted as Mowry City, although there is apparently no evidence that, other than the use of his name, Mowry was an investor or developer of the village that bore his name. Of interest is the fact that Bartlett and the Boundary Commission camped April 30 to May 1, 1851, at or near the place on the Mimbres River that would eventually become Mowry City. Virtually nothing remains of Mowry City, the site having been incorporated into the headquarters of a ranch. However, there is a ghost town of Mowry in the Patagonia Mountains of southern Arizona; it consists mostly of crumbling adobe walls and is located immediately adjacent to the still active Mowry Mine. See L. Boyd Finch, *A Southwestern Land Scam: The 1859 Report of the Mowry City Association* (Tucson: Friends of the University of Arizona Library, 1990).

65. The Old State House where Bartlett served as Secretary of State is a red brick and brownstone building that was constructed in the 1760s on a hillside to the east of the Providence River. At the time of its construction, the front of the Old State House and its main entrance were oriented to the west, overlooking North Main Street at the base of the hill. As a result of nineteenth-century renovations, the Old State House was internally reoriented to the east, and the building took its address on Benefit

FIGURE 29

Street, the street immediately adjacent to the rear of the building. Thus, the Old State House operated for many years with two entrances, and its modern address is 150 Benefit Street (see Fig. 29).

The Old State House was succeeded by the new Rhode Island State House, an impressive marble structure that opened on Smith Hill in 1901. The former seat of government was then converted into the Sixth District Courthouse, which functioned on the site until the 1970s. Today, the Old State House is on the National Register of Historic Places and is part of the College Hill Historic Landmark District. Currently, the Rhode Island Historical Preservation and Heritage Commission occupies the building.

According to Providence directories, Bartlett lived at several locations during his tenure as Secretary of State from 1855 to 1872, including 147 Benefit Street in 1862 and 1865. All of his residences from this period were conveniently located within walking distance of the Old State House, the Providence Athenaeum, Brown University, and the Nightingale-Brown House, which was the residence of John Carter Brown.

66. The reference here is to George Henry Corliss (1817–1888), president and founder of the Corliss Steam Engine Company in Providence, Rhode Island. Corliss was best known for his invention of a special valve employed on steam engines of the era, and the efficiency of his engines was displayed not only in Paris, but also

---

FIGURE 29 (*opposite*). The front of the Old State House, a brick and stone building that faces away from its present address at 150 Benefit Street in Providence. This view is from the west, and the photo was taken along an incline that leads to North Main Street. As Rhode Island's Secretary of State, Bartlett had his office in this building from 1855 to 1872. It was here that Bartlett compiled and published many of the state's colonial records. All of Bartlett's residences from 1854 onwards were on or near Benefit Street, conveniently located within easy walking distance of the State House. Photo by Jerry E. Mueller.

at other exhibitions, including the Centennial Exposition held in Philadelphia in 1876. At the latter, his behemoth double-piston steam engine employed a 30-foot diameter flywheel and was able to power all of the other equipment in Machinery Hall. Corliss received many prestigious awards in his lifetime, especially for his work on steam engines, although he also invented numerous other mechanical devices. Virtually nothing remains of the old Corliss Company that was located east of the Providence and Worcester Railroad tracks and west of Corliss Street, in north Providence. What is preserved from the era of George Corliss is his Victorian mansion built in 1875–1882 at 45 Prospect Street, a structure known today as the Corliss-Brackett House, wherein resides the Admissions Office of Brown University. For illustrations of Corliss and the giant double steam engine that was displayed in Philadelphia in 1876, see Robert C. Post, editor, *1876: A Centennial Exhibition* (Washington, D.C.: National Museum of History and Technology, Smithsonian Institution, 1976); and William D. Sawyer, *Corliss: Man and Engine*, in *Stationary Power*, no. 10, 1994, the International Stationary Steam Engine Society.

67. Bartlett was agitated for many years by the failure of the Federal government to reimburse him for what he believed were reasonable and proper expenses he had incurred while he was U.S. Boundary Commissioner. It appears the Democratic administration of Franklin Pierce had little sympathy for Bartlett's cause, inasmuch as these debts were in part cost overruns on a project that Bartlett had been hired to direct under the previous administrations of Zachary Taylor and Millard Fillmore. Although Bartlett's days as Boundary Commissioner ended abruptly in March 1853, his *Journal of Finances, U. S. Boundary Commission* contains entries and adjustments of his accounts well into 1861 (MSS 286–John Russell Bartlett Papers, Box 1, Folder 14, Rhode Island Historical Society Library).

Additional claims and requests from former Boundary Commission employees for back wages, expenses, etc., continued into the 1870s. It appears that this very problem might have ended Bartlett's decades-old intimate friendship with Thomas H. Webb, who served as physician and secretary on the Boundary Commission for two and one-half years. In a letter to Bartlett dated April 15, 1861, Webb relates that he understands through another former commission employee, Henry Jacobs, that Bartlett had effected a settlement of his Boundary Commission affairs with the government. "I suppose, this being the case, there is nothing now in the way of my obtaining the back dues for Secretary's services, etc." In another letter to Bartlett dated July 6, 1861, Webb seems irritated that Bartlett has ignored Webb's request in the letter of April 15. The next, and last, letter in the Bartlett files from Webb is dated November 22, 1861. Webb says he received Bartlett's letters of April 17 and July 9, 1861, in which Bartlett apparently promised payment in September, but nothing had been received. In a terse comment, Webb writes, "oblige me by making an early remittance." (These letters are in the Bartlett Papers at the John Carter Brown Library.)

68. There are several letters from Theresa Yelverton to Bartlett among the Bartlett Papers at the John Carter Brown Library. One of her undated letters, filed under January 1867 (the date is probably incorrect), indicates she had a pleasant time during her visit to Providence and would like to return. At the time, she was giving readings at Irving Hall in New York. There are additional letters from her dated October 1867, the month Bartlett returned from his trip to Europe.

69. William Jones Hoppin was a lawyer, diplomat, and author who spent much of his adult life in Europe. He was one of many Hoppins from Providence with whom Bartlett appears to have had a long and cordial relationship. A brother, Augustus Hoppin, was a well known artist, illustrator, and author, who drew several caricature-like sketches of scenes from the Southwest that Bartlett included in *Personal Narrative* in 1854. Augustus, along with Bartlett, was a member of a select group of Providence men

who belonged to the local Friday Evening Club. A cousin to William and Augustus was William W. Hoppin, with whom Bartlett
was acquainted in the early 1830s when the Providence Athenaeum was being formed and when both men were members of
the Franklin Society. The latter Hoppin would later serve as governor of Rhode Island, with John Russell Bartlett as his Secretary
of State (1855–1857). When Bartlett was not renominated by his
party in 1872, he wrote to his former governor and colleague:

> I thank you most sincerely for the great interest you have taken
> on my behalf since the Republican Convention dropped my name
> as Secretary of State.... I must look upon the result as a conse-
> quence, which may at any time, attend the holder of any public
> office. For years past many have said to me "you will probably
> hold your office as long as you desire," but I have always said in
> reply that some political combination in my own party might be
> the means of depriving me of office, without regard to the faith-
> ful manner in which I had performed my duties. Perhaps it is all
> for the best, at least I shall think so. (Bartlett to W. W. Hoppin,
> March 23, 1872, MSS 493–Hoppin Papers, Rhode Island Historical
> Society Library.)

70. In a handwritten document dated February 3, 1904, William
Weeden states that the Friday Evening Club was organized on
January 16, 1868, for the purpose of social meetings and the discussion of literary, philosophical, aesthetic, historical, and scientific subjects. Also, the club apparently consisted of approximately fifteen members and met fortnightly during the winter
season. According to the club's 16th *Annual Report* dated January
4, 1884, the organization started the previous year with 12 members and had lost one, and a total of 11 meetings were held. On
March 14, 1884, club member, George Ide Chace, retired physi-
cist at Brown University, wrote the following note to Bartlett:

> Will you go with me to the club, this evening? I shall take a car-
> riage, and will call for you at 7¼ P.M., so you need not reply to

this. It is the last meeting of the season, and as I read, I do not care to fatigue myself by walking through the mud. I shall order the carriage to come for me at 11½ O'clock.

Bartlett maintained lists of the papers presented by himself and others. In the case of Professor E. W. Blake, Bartlett records, "Electric Light" (February 27, 1880); "Color Blindness" (March 1, 1881); "Sun Spots" (March 16, 1882); and, "A Glimpse of Ranch Life in Wyoming Territory" (February 10, 1882). Several of the actual papers read by Bartlett are preserved in the records of the club. These manuscripts are all relatively short and display immaculate penmanship: "Phenicia and the Phenicians" (3 pages, undated); "Psychic Force and the Phantom World" (3 pages, undated); "Arctic Geography" (4 pages, undated); "Pompeii and Herculaneum" (2 pages, January 17, 1873); "Etruria and the Etruscans" (3 pages, January 2, 1874); and "The Aryan Race, its Languages, Literature and Migrations" (3 pages, November 23, 1877). Also preserved in the club records is a one-page statement by Bartlett on the existence of a personal God, and a note that suggests he gave a paper entitled, "Antiquity of Man—Archeology, or archy [archeology] tending into history."

The following list provides a more complete description of the papers Bartlett presented to the Friday Evening Club, with the additional information taken from Bartlett's personal records deposited with the club. The entries and their titles are given in chronological order.

"The Swiss Lake Dwellings and prehistoric history of Man." October 1867.

"Prehistoric Man and His Contemporaries." General account. January 31, 1868.

"Prehistoric Man and His Contemporaries, with an account of recent discoveries." December 18, 1868.

"Cuneiform Inscriptions, chiefly from among the ruins of Babylon and Nineveh." December 17 or December 30, 1869.

"Studies of Ancient Egypt and of late discoveries in Egyptian literature." December 30, 1870.

"The Old Runic Northern Monuments of Scandinavia." December 8, 1871.

"Pompeii and Herculaneum; including an account of my visit to those ancient cities in 1872." January 17, 1873.

"Ancient Etruria and the Etruscans." January 1874.

"Psychic Force and the Phantom World." January 21, 1875.

" Phenicia and the Phonicians." December 1875.

"Arctic Geography, with account of attempts for the discovery of a North West and North East Passage, and of efforts to reach the North Pole." December 8, 1876.

"The Aryan Race, its Languages, Literature and Migrations." November 3, 1877.

"Sanscrit Language and Literature, with an account of the Zend and old Persian languages." Not presented.

"The earliest appearance of man on the Earth. Recent discoveries in the United States relating thereto—with the present state of the question." December 6, 1878.

"The Libraries of the Ancients; including those of Egypt, Assyria, Greece and Rome." December 19, 1879.

"The Exodus of the Israelites from Egypt. The new views of their route as suggested by Henry Brugsch Bey." December 3, 1880.

"The Cave and Rock Cut Temples of India." November 18, 1881.

"Bibliographers, Bibliophiles and Bibliomaniacs." November 24, 1882.

"Views of the most ancient people regarding immortality and the future life." February 1, 1884.

For additional information, see MSS 431–Friday Evening Club Records, Rhode Island Historical Society Library.

In Box 13 of Bartlett's Miscellaneous Papers at the John Carter Brown Library are several manuscripts that Bartlett apparently read to local organizations. The earliest, entitled "Babylon," is 35 pages long and was read in November 1854. Assigned to the 1860s is a manuscript for which pages 1–38 deal with "Egypt;" pages 39–50 are missing; and pages 51–72 discuss "Antiquities." Also assigned to the 1860s are two papers of 27 and 26 pages respectively, the second being the continuation of the first, on "Egyptian Antiquities." It is possible that the Egyptian manuscripts, even if read in the 1860s, were derived or rewritten from much earlier works by Bartlett.

71. Bartlett's entry number 11 lists the author as Campbell, but this attribution is likely a mistake. In his chapter on "Hon. John R. Bartlett's Library," in *Private Libraries of Providence* (Providence: Sidney S. Rider, 1878), Horatio Rogers indicates that Bartlett possessed two extra-illustrated books on Mary, Queen of Scots, one by Petit, which is number 10 on Bartlett's list, and the other by Chalmers. Undoubtedly, Rogers's reference is to author George Chalmers and his 1818 edition of *The Life of Mary, Queen of Scots*, published in two volumes. Thus, it is a virtual certainty that Bartlett's entry in item number 11 should read "Chalmers" instead of "Campbell." The John Hay Library at Brown University holds two copies of Chalmers's book, and in the library's card catalog is the following notation: "Copy 1 is 30 cm. and has added throughout text, plates (part. mounted, part. fold.) collected from various sources relating to Mary, Queen of Scots." Is this the same copy that was extra-illustrated by Bartlett?

Rogers also indicates (p. 144) that Bartlett extra-illustrated and possessed "Wiffen's Memoirs of the House of Russell, with nearly two hundred portraits," a volume that does not appear on Bartlett's list. The reference here must be to Jeremiah H. Wiffen,

Historical Memoirs of the House of Russell; From the Time of the Norman Conquest, published in two volumes in 1833.

72. Frances Sargent Locke Osgood was a popular American poetess who resided in New York City during the decade of the 1840s, the same general period that Bartlett & Welford operated their bookstore on Broadway. It appears from a number of accounts that Poe and Osgood enjoyed a particularly close relationship, as is suggested by Bartlett's comment, but whether that relationship was ever more than admiration or flirtation is open to debate and speculation. In a recent book, *Poe and Fanny*, it is suggested that theirs was an illicit relationship, one that even produced an offspring. However, if the conservative Bartletts had known or suspected such was the case, it is extremely doubtful they would have given the name, Fanny Osgood Bartlett, to their youngest daughter, who was born in 1850, the same year that her namesake died. For more on Poe and Osgood, see Mary G. DeJong, "Her Fair Fame: The Reputation of Frances Sargent Osgood, Woman Poet," in *Studies in the American Renaissance*, 1987, pp. 265–283, and John May, *Poe and Fanny* (Chapel Hill: Algonquin Books, 2004).

73. During a portion of their stay in London, the Bartletts enjoyed the company of John Russell Bartlett, Jr., and his wife, Jeanie, even sharing a parlor as part of their accommodations. On page 3 of his diary of the trip to Europe, Bartlett states, "Very pleasant to have five of our family again sitting at the same table." Bartlett also renewed acquaintance in London with his former bookstore partner, Charles Welford, as he had on his earlier trip to Europe. A humorous incident during their London stay occurred when Ellen visited the Zoological Gardens and had a rose stolen from her hat by a monkey. A major omission in Bartlett's account of this trip is his subsequent travel to Switzerland, Germany, Belgium, and Italy, although this part of his itinerary is detailed in his trip diary held by the John Carter Brown Library.

74. There are many English translations of *Ode to God*. The one that Bartlett cites can be found on pages 3–4 of *Specimens of the Russian*

Poets, translated by John Bowring (London, 1821), 2nd edition.
The first stanza in its entirety is:

> O Thou eternal One! Whose presence bright
> All space doth occupy, all motion guide;
> Unchanged through time's all-devastating flight;
> Thou only God! There is no God Beside!
> Being above all things! Three in One!
> Whom none can comprehend and none explore;
> Who fill'st existence with *Thyself* alone:
> Embracing all,—supporting,—ruling o'er,—
> Being whom we call God—and know no more!

75. It is somewhat puzzling why Bartlett decided to write out the whole of the Gettysburg Address in his autobiography. Equally puzzling is the fact that this account differs slightly from the more commonly accepted versions, suggesting that Bartlett might have written out the address from memory. For other renditions of the Gettysburg address derived from Lincoln's spoken and written texts, see Garry Wills, *Lincoln at Gettysburg: The Words That Remade America* (New York: Simon & Schuster, 1992).

76. The Prince of Wales at this time was Albert Edward, the son of Queen Victoria and Prince Albert. Albert Edward and his entourage reached Quebec aboard the *Hero* on August 18, 1860. He would later travel to Montreal, Ottawa, Toronto, Niagara Falls, Detroit, Chicago, St. Louis, Washington, Philadelphia, New York, Boston, New Hampshire, and Maine, leaving North America for England on October 22, 1860. In 1901, Albert Edward would succeed his mother on the throne of England under the title, King Edward VII. See Stanley Weintraub, *Edward the Caresser: The Playboy Prince Who Became Edward VII* (New York: The Free Press, 2001).

INDEX

INDEX

Page numbers in italics refer to illustrations that depict the entry. Parenthetical expressions denote the relationship of the entry to John Russell Bartlett (JRB) unless otherwise specified.

PRINTED UNDER THE SUPERVISION OF
MARTINO MARDERSTEIG AT STAMPERIA VALDONEGA
ARBIZZANO DI VERONA, ITALY

BOUND BY
LEGATORIA ZANARDI GROUP, PADOVA, ITALY
IN MANIFATTURA DEL SEVESO
CIALUX CLOTH

DESIGNED AND COMPOSED BY
MARK ARGETSINGER
ROCHESTER, NEW YORK